THE $50,000 STOVE HANDLE

Also by Gordon Pape

Financial Advice

Building Wealth in the '90s

Retiring Wealthy

Low-Risk Investing

Buyer's Guide to Mutual Funds

Buyer's Guide to RRSPs

Fiction
(with Tony Aspler)

Chain Reaction

The Scorpion Sanction

The Music Wars

Non-Fiction
(with Donna Gabeline and Dane Lanken)

Montreal at the Crossroads

THE $50,000 STOVE HANDLE
AND OTHER PERILS OF HOME IMPROVEMENTS

GORDON PAPE

Illustrated by
Kendrew Pape

HOUNSLOW

The $50,000 Stove Handle
and Other Perils of Home Improvements

Publishers: Kirk Howard & Anthony Hawke
Editor: Shirley Knight Morris
Designer: Gerard Williams
Desktop production: Dennis Mills
Printer: Best Gagné Book Manufacturers Inc.

Front cover illustration: Gerard Williams
Interior illustrations: Kendrew Pape

Canadian Cataloguing in Publication Data
Pape, Gordon, 1936-
    The $50,000 stove handle and other perils of home improvements

ISBN 0-88882-164-6

1. Dwellings - Remodeling - Humor. 2. Canadian wit and humor
(English).* I. Title.

PS8581.A74F5   1993   643'.7'0207   C93-094607-3
PR9199.3.P37F5   1993

Publication was assisted by the Canada Council, the Department of
Communications, and the Ontario Publishing Centre of the Ontario
Ministry of Culture, Tourism and Recreation.

Hounslow Press
A subsidiary of Dundurn Press Limited
2181 Queen Street East, Suite 301
Toronto, Ontario, Canada M4E 1E5

Printed and bound in Canada

Author's Note

All the events described in this book actually took place; however, in some cases I have telescoped the time frames. Also, several of the characters mentioned are composites, although all the members of my own family are real.

I would like to thank especially Beth Lawrence of Laney Interiors for her help in the preparation of this book and for her invaluable assistance in transforming our house into a true home. I would also like to thank all the good tradespeople who worked with us in making it happen. Special thanks to my son, Kendrew, for the illustrations that help bring the pages that follow to life. And, most of all, I want to thank my wife, Shirley – not only for bringing it all together – but for remembering the little details that served to make this book possible.

Gordon Pape
Toronto, Ont.
April, 1993

Preface

It was hate at first sight.

From the street, the house seemed to be all garage. I had visions of sleeping in a loft over the car.

Compared to the elegant Cape Cod home we were leaving in Beaconsfield, a suburb of Montreal, it looked like a tacky suburban box.

Which it was.

The back yard was dark, overhung by giant trees that appeared to have been recently transplanted from the Amazon – our contribution to saving the rain forests.

The lot itself was minuscule, a postage stamp compared to the acre we were leaving behind.

It did have the advantage of a ravine immediately behind – with a rushing stream that my wife, Shirley, could envisage sweeping away our young children on a stormy day.

The rickety back deck looked as though a stiff breeze would bring it tumbling down. That fear was later verified – the deck quivered whenever the dog walked across it.

The inside of the house wasn't bad, if you like dark brown kitchens, pink bathrooms, and shower stalls that pour water into the room immediately below.

And the price! Almost twice as much as we were getting for our beautiful Montreal home. Moving to Toronto was clearly going to drive me into bankruptcy!

Oh, we saw better places. One or two we actually liked. But the cost! A hundred and seventy-five thousand for a two-story colonial home in the fashionable York Mills area. Sure, it came complete with a swimming pool, billiards table and even a mini projection room. But who could afford a palace like that?

Perhaps I forgot to mention the year was 1975. Palaces were cheaper then.

We didn't have much time to make up our minds. The company that was uprooting us from our fabulous Montreal home – the one I'd promised my wife only twenty months earlier we'd live in for at least twenty years – that company was only paying for one weekend visit to Toronto for the two of us. That should be adequate time to make the most expensive purchase decision of your life. Shouldn't it?

So we settled on the house on Woodsworth Road. My wife fought it all the way. But it was the only place within our already stretched price range that wasn't either unthinkable, undesirable, or located on the far fringes of the universe, in places like Scarborough.

It's only temporary, we rationalized. My career as a journalist had me switching cities an average of once every three and a half years. Why should this time be any different?

Thirteen years later, we decided it was time to do something about our "temporary" residence. The kids had almost grown up. Kimberley was off to university, Kendrew was about to start, and Deborah was a year away.

We had a little money saved and it was time to move to the kind of home we'd always wanted. Something like the house we'd left behind in Beaconsfield.

As a first step, we had our little place valued. "Put it on the market at five thirty-five," the agent said. "You should get close to that."

This was 1988, the Toronto real estate market was still hot, so that figure didn't seem unreasonable. Since we had paid one hundred and twenty-nine thousand for the house back in 1975 – at the time, a fortune – we even felt pretty pleased with ourselves.

So we went shopping for the first time in years. We looked at a new mega-home which had been squeezed into a lot about the size of ours just a few blocks away.

Impressive, sort of, if winding staircases, cathedral ceilings and a twelve-lane expressway a block away turn you on. Certainly the price was impressive. Over one and a half million.

"Do you realize," I said as we drove home, "that even if we got full price for our house, we'd have to take out a million dollar mortgage? A million dollar mortgage!" Shirley glumly stared out of the car window.

When we got home, I checked my mortgage tables. At twelve per cent interest (the prevailing rate at that time), the monthly carrying cost would be over ten thousand dollars!

I suggested we set our sights a little lower.

We did. The next place we looked at cost only one and

a quarter million. A six hundred and fifty thousand dollar mortgage! Monthly carrying costs of more than six thousand six hundred!

I began to suspect that the only people who could afford such homes were dentists and drug dealers.

"What about renovating our place?" I asked as we drove home.

"I suggested that last year," Shirley sweetly reminded me. "You said it would cost too much."

"How much?"

"At least a quarter million."

"What a bargain! When do we start?"

Bargains are rarely as good as they first seem. There were to be times in the ensuing years that the idea of a million dollar mortgage didn't seem so terrible after all. If only I had known then . . .

Contents

Preface / vii

The $50,000 Stove Handle / 1

The Misha Factor / 12

The Dog's Stamping on the Deck Again / 21

Why Is My Hair Freezing? / 31

What Do You Do With a Pregnant Groundhog? / 43

The Designer Knows Best (Sometimes) / 57

It Costs What? / 65

Guess What, Mike, The Ceiling's Leaking Again / 71

Pack the Fish Dear, We're Moving / 78

The Wine Cellar from Hell / 92

Buy a Dog, Fix It Up / 104

How We'll Do It Next Time / 112

The $50,000 Stove Handle

The decision on where we would begin was made the day the stove handle came off.

I didn't realize the significance of it at the time. I was busy reading a cereal box, trying to figure out if the sugar content of the oat bran offset its cholesterol-reducing advantages.

(When I was a kid, I used to read cereal boxes to see what kind of great prize I could get by mailing off the box top and twenty-five cents. Now I read them to see if what's inside is liable to kill me.)

While I was engrossed in deciphering ingredients, Shirley was warming muffins. I heard her mutter "shig", or something to that effect.

I glanced over. She was holding the oven handle. The problem was, she was nowhere near the stove.

"It came off," she said.

"Guess you'll have to call someone to fix it," I observed, returning to the delights of the cereal box.

"Umm," she said.

That got my attention. I've lived with Shirley long enough to know that a non-committal grunt does not imply assent.

"I don't think so," she said thoughtfully.

"What?"

"I don't think I'll call in someone to fix the handle."

"You think you can do it yourself?" I'm about as much use around the house as a fur salesman at an environmentalists' convention. If something has to be fixed, it's up to Shirley.

"No."

"Oh. I get it. You want a new stove. Well, that one is about twenty years old, so I suppose. . ."

"No."

"No?"

"I want one of those stove tops."

"But that would mean a wall oven too. We'd have to remodel that whole area."

"No."

"We wouldn't?"

"No. Because I don't want it there."

"Where do you want it?"

"Over there. Where the door is." She pointed to the side door that dominated the north wall of the kitchen.

"But that would mean. . ."

"Exactly. You said we were going to renovate the house. This is where we'll start."

Oh well, I thought. What can a few changes to the kitchen cost?

Would you believe more than fifty thousand dollars? There's something about kitchens – once you start spending, you can't stop.

I'd already had a taste of that. A year or so earlier, one of our taps had sprung a leak. Shirley couldn't handle it so we picked a plumber from the yellow pages and called for help.

He was Italian. He fussed around with the faucet for a bit and then announced that it was finished. Beyond repair. It would have to be replaced. It would cost three hundred dollars.

I swallowed hard.

"But there is more," the plumber said with a doleful look. "I don't like what I see underneath. The water, she has been leaking for a long time. I call my friend to help. He is carpenter."

The friend arrived within an hour. He was also from Italy. While we watched, the two poked and prodded and jabbered at each other in Italian.

When they were finished, they both looked woebegone.

"Is not good news, sir," the plumber announced. "The water, she has rotted the wood all around. It will have to be fixed."

"What does that mean?"

Downcast eyes. Great sadness.

"The counter – it will have to be replaced."

"What will that cost?"

"About a thousand dollars."

"I see."

"There's more." I thought he was going to burst into tears. The carpenter stared at the ceiling.

"More?"

"The sink. She won't fit in the new counter. You will

need a new one."

"How much?"

"Maybe five, six hundred."

I began to suspect the main source of revenue for the Mafia isn't drugs or rackets at all – it's plumbing.

As if to confirm my suspicions, the carpenter suddenly chimed in.

"Of course, you can't just replace that part of the counter. It will all have to be done. New surfaces all around."

I was trying to digest all this when Shirley jumped in.

"Forget it," she instructed. "Replace the tap. Shore up the rotten wood wherever necessary. And that's it. No more. Finito."

The Italians looked as if they'd been struck by lightning. I stared at my wife. Pass up an opportunity for a whole new kitchen counter? Was she ill?

I didn't know then about the secret file folder – the one she'd been using to collect magazine articles, pictures, brochures and anything else she could lay her hands on about kitchens. She had decided exactly what she wanted and she wasn't about to let these two characters muck it up.

But now she was ready. The fateful file appeared. Lovingly, she showed me pictures of spice drawers, wine racks, stained glass display cases, built-in lazy susans, bread drawers, breakfast counters, cookbook cases, hide-away towel racks, built-in wall ovens, stove tops, pop-out waste pails, under-counter lights, water purifiers, side-by-side fridge/ freezers with water and ice dispensers, garbage compactors and more.

"And which of these do you want in your kitchen?" I asked naively.

"All of them."

I shuddered.

The first step in having a kitchen re-done is figuring out how you're going to live without a stove, fridge, sink and other little niceties during the weeks it takes to complete the work.

That means you should never schedule the job for the

winter, unless you happen to live in Florida. A barbecue can take the place of a stove in the summer months, but it's not much use when the wind is howling and it's minus ten outside.

The second is to have the work done when most of your family is planning to be somewhere else. The fewer mouths to feed, the better.

Using these two guidelines, Shirley worked out her plan. Our oldest daughter, Kimberley, planned to go back to university in the fall for post-graduate work. Our son, Kendrew, would be starting his first year of college. That meant two of the kids would be gone by mid-September, leaving only Shirley, me, and our youngest daughter, Deborah.

Three, Shirley figured she could handle. We'd use the bar in the family room as a temporary base, equipping it with a microwave, electric frying pan and toaster. The barbecue would be outside. It would all work out just fine. She called the contractor in May to set the date.

One of the joys of having children is that they rarely do what you expect of them. This unpredictability keeps things lively – but it can also screw up the most carefully laid plans.

First, it was Kimberley. She'd had enough of university, she told us after her convocation. To heck with the post-graduate work. She was coming home.

Not only that, but she was bringing her boyfriend with her. Not to live, of course. But he would be coming into town frequently to visit. Of course we could have him over for dinner, couldn't we?

Shirley's face turned white.

Then Kendrew received a letter. It was from an old school friend who had moved to Australia a few years previously. She was going to be working in England for the summer and returning home by way of Canada. She would love to spend some time in Toronto seeing all her old mates again. Was there any chance we could put her up for a couple of weeks? She would be arriving in September.

Shirley turned ashen. But we knew the family well, and we had an extra bed. We could hardly say no.

Kendrew was elated and announced he would be coming into town every weekend she was visiting to see her.

Suddenly our makeshift kitchen was going to have to feed up to seven people a day! I awaited September with trepidation.

The first person to arrive on the designated morning was the man they call "The Wrecker". Every contractor has one. His job was to go into our kitchen with a crowbar and wreak as much devastation as he could in the shortest possible time.

This was a man who clearly loved his work. We sat downstairs (our house is a back-split with the kitchen on the upper level) and listened, appalled, to the ripping, tearing and smashing noises that emerged. When he finally stopped for lunch, we went in and surveyed the scene. The pantry shelves had been ripped out and lay in splinters on the floor. The countertops had been reduced to chunks of jagged Arborite. Cupboard doors were strewn everywhere. Worst of all, the new Moen faucet that we'd paid the Italian plumber three hundred dollars for barely a year earlier lay discarded on a trash heap. I could have wept.

The next day he brought down the ceiling in a roar of plaster dust. Our kitchen looked as if it had just been hit by a mortar shell.

The Wrecker smiled and said goodbye. His job was done. As he left, I wondered what kind of training was necessary for a job like that. Six months planting bombs for the IRA, I decided.

To build a new kitchen from scratch, you need to employ a variety of tradespeople. Some are a pleasure to work with. Others can be creeps.

Our electrician fell into the latter category.

Electricians tend to regard themselves as being among the elite of the construction trades, almost on a level with plumbers. The electrician assigned to our kitchen, a man in his early twenties with a strong macho streak, had let this exalted status go to his head.

First, he argued with our designer, Beth. The diagrams

weren't complete enough. The potlights were in the wrong places. The plug positions weren't right. Beth, who stands about five foot three, came over and had it out with the six-footer in the middle of the shell that had been our kitchen. Hell hath no fury like a designer scorned!

"The diagrams are perfectly fine for your needs," she told him. "You're the electrician. It's up to you to figure out how to set up the wiring to make it happen. Or is that beyond you?"

Everything was installed as she had instructed.

That scene didn't faze our obnoxious electrician, how-ever. He immediately started to pick on someone else. Make a mess from drilling? He'd demand the carpenter clean it up. Extra pieces of wire? Someone else could toss them in the trash can. A dirty job crawling through attic insulation to run wiring? His apprentice got it.

His attitude so disturbed Shirley that she finally had the temerity to ask him why he didn't clean up his own messes.

He looked astonished that anyone could suggest such a thing and turned his back on her.

Someone that unpleasant had better be perfection at his work. He wasn't. When our cabinet maker discovered the electrician had failed to install proper protective covers for two high-powered display lights, he gleefully brought the error to our attention. The electrician had to come back and put it all right – which meant going up into the attic himself, since his apprentice wasn't along. He emerged complaining and covered with insulation. Justice had been done.

The carpenter was the exact opposite. He was amiable, helpful and highly professional at his work – the man the entire project revolved around. His name was Irish – Pat – but he must have spent some time in Quebec because every time he hit his finger with a hammer or scratched himself he would unleash a string of French-Canadian oaths that would make Madonna blush. Perhaps he thought no one else would understand them. We did.

Pat needed to be kick-started with two cups of coffee

every morning and chain-smoked his way through the rest of the day. But he was a solid worker who took great pride in dong things right. When he finished his stint and said good-bye, Shirley felt it was like the captain leaving the ship. I just hoped the ship wasn't going to sink.

Many tradespeople have the annoying habit of bringing along their own radios and tuning them to the station that plays the most aggravating music on the dial. Hammers, drills and power saws are bad enough; mix in heavy metal played at high volume and it's enough to convince anyone it's time to take the dog for a walk.

Our cabinet maker was a little different though. Oh, he brought along his own radio like everyone else. But he tuned it to CBC-FM and went around all day whistling classical music. What a relief! Unfortunately, his job was over in a few days.

In the hierarchy of the building trades, the tile man occupies a special place. He's not like the others, you see. They're workers. He's an artist. And artists are, by nature, temperamental.

I assume that not all tile men are Italian, but certainly all those we've dealt with have been. Perhaps Italians are the only ones with the flair and creativity needed to create the kind of ceramic tapestries that grace many homes.

Shirley had been warned about Luigi before he ever appeared.

"Don't say anything to make him mad," the construction foreman had told her. "If there's any problem, don't complain to him. Tell me about it."

The day Luigi was to arrive, we waited fearfully. He didn't come.

"Jury duty," the foreman explained when we called. "The trial's lasting longer than expected. I hope he'll be out in time to finish your job before he leaves for Italy. He's going for three months."

Luigi arrived two days later, grumbling about the legal system that had made him weeks behind in his work.

He scowled at us, scowled at the three-quarters finished kitchen, scowled at his apprentice and went to inspect the tiles Shirley and Beth had chosen.

He came back looking content. They'd purchased Italian tiles. From then on, there was never a problem with him.

Not even when the moment of truth came – applying the decorative tiles to the kitchen walls.

Beth and Shirley knew exactly how they wanted them arranged. They wanted to supervise the work. The foreman was appalled.

"Be very careful how you put it to him," he advised. "Don't question his competence in any way. Don't suggest he could do anything but a wonderful job. Just say something like you think it might be fun to help out."

They were quaking when they broached the idea to Luigi. He just shrugged and said: "Sure." When the work was finished, they praised it to the skies. He didn't smile exactly. But at least he stopped scowling for a moment. Maybe it was because he was leaving for Italy the next night.

Shirley had decided from the beginning she wanted Corian counters in the kitchen. She had fallen in love with the smooth seamlessness of the material. Never mind that it cost hundreds of dollars more. How often did she get a new kitchen, after all?

We had no idea what was involved in installing Corian, nor did we ask when we ordered. Big mistake.

I should have been tipped off when the workmen sealed off the doors to the kitchen with plastic sheeting and donned protective masks. But it was only when I glanced in a couple of hours after they began work that I understood their precautions.

My initial thought was that it was somehow snowing in the kitchen; then I realized I was looking at fine particles of Corian suspended in the air.

I suddenly understood how that seamless effect is achieved: intensive shaving and sanding that leaves your home coated with a white dust for weeks afterwards.

Weeks? We were still finding pockets of the stuff two

years later. It settled on our furniture. It clogged our air ducts. It coated our dishes. It collected in drawers. Lord knows what it did to our lungs. Having Mount Vesuvius dump a load of volcanic ash on your home couldn't have been much worse.

Oh yeah – the counters look great.

The last major task before the kitchen was complete was to sand, stain and apply urethane to the new flooring. The job was complicated by the fact the entrance hall of the house had to be done at the same time.

That hall is the only access to the living room, bedrooms and main bathroom. We were told that we wouldn't be able to walk across it for three days. It seemed that our only choice was to move out or be trapped downstairs in the family room for that length of time. Neither prospect was particularly appealing.

We confronted the floor man. He examined the situation from all angles and came up with an idea.

We could set up a ladder on the stair landing and use it to climb over the top of the railing into the dining room. (If this sounds confusing, keep in mind we have a very unusual house. The stairwell is right in the centre of the building and is open on the dining room side. Perhaps they designed it that way so mothers could lean over the dining room railing and call the kids up to bed.)

Once we were in the dining room, we could then walk through the living room to the entrance hall. By taking one broad step across it, we could reach the bedroom hallway and be home free.

The kids thought it was a great plan. Shirley and I were dubious. The idea of scaling ladders and climbing over railings just to go to the bathroom seemed rather daunting. Shirley suggested we sign up for mountain goat training.

But it was that or move out. The ladder was set up, the floor man went to work, and I spent the next few days learning the fine arts of bladder control. I began to envy the dog. All we had to do was open the back door and there was his bathroom! Not a ladder in sight.

And then it was all over. The appliances were delivered and installed and the kitchen was pronounced ready. It was only two weeks late – not bad by renovation standards. Shirley declared it to be perfect and announced that if we ever moved again, she intended to take it with her.

I just breathed a sigh of relief that the ordeal was over. Little did I know!

The Misha Factor

I've always loved dogs.

I'm not exactly sure why. One of my earliest memories is of Snookie, our temperamental Yorkshire Terrier, warning me away from her food dish with a snarl.

That should have been enough to make me a lifetime

dog-hater, but it wasn't. When Snookie went to doggie paradise (at least, that's where my mother said she went; I remember thinking at the time it was too good for her), I began agitating immediately for a replacement.

It didn't happen right away – my mother mumbled something about me being trouble enough. But then Pepper showed up.

He appeared at our back door one day – we were living in a country home in Michigan at the time. What immediately caught my attention was the unusual way he urinated – while standing on his two front legs! I'd never seen anything like it – still haven't to this day.

My mother opined that he was a circus dog that had either escaped or been abandoned. He certainly hadn't learned by himself to stand on his forelegs while peeing.

She warned me not to give him any food or he'd keep hanging around. Naturally, as soon as her back was turned, I slipped him part of my lunch. Pepper never left us for the rest of his life.

I delighted in his versatility – it turned out he could also walk a considerable distance on his back legs and perform several other unusual tricks. I charged the neighbourhood kids a nickel to see him perform and gave the money to my mother to show her how valuable he was.

But Pepper was an old dog when we got him. I longed for a puppy.

The opportunity arose when my father returned home from one of his frequent lengthy trips. A friend's bitch had just given birth. The pups were mutts and they were giving them away. Would I like to see them?

My mother scowled. "We already have a dog," she noted.

"We're just going to look," I said.

We came back with Ginger.

How could anyone have resisted him? The pups were a Collie/Labrador cross. Ginger had twinkly brown eyes, a mouth that looked as if it were perpetually smiling and boundless energy. A perfect companion for an eight-year-old only child.

Pepper wasn't amused. He regarded Ginger as an unwelcome intruder and immediately put the puppy in his place by snapping at him whenever he came near. Fortunately, at this point, Pepper had no teeth left so the damage to the pup was minimal.

In time, they learned to co-exist. Ginger became dutifully respectful of the older dog and Pepper responded with grudging tolerance. They both slept at the bottom of my bed at night, each in his own spot. I loved them dearly.

One of the most traumatic days of my life was the day Ginger was killed. Living as we did in a rural area, I had to take a bus to school. The pick-up point was about a mile away from our home.

Ginger would accompany me on the walk (Pepper was too old at this point). Occasionally, he would race alongside the bus after I got on – I imagined it was because he wanted to come with me. The bus driver thought this was great sport and would accelerate to see how fast Ginger could go. I think he once topped thirty miles an hour!

On that sad day, Ginger started running alongside the bus as usual and the driver stepped on the gas; then the dog did something I'd never seen before. He cut directly in front of the bus. I still remember watching terrified as Ginger stopped in his tracks and looked up at us, just as the bus hit him. He died instantly. He was two years old.

Even Pepper seemed distressed. For weeks afterwards, he would sniff at Ginger's spot at the foot of the bed every night before settling down. He lived to a very old age and I loved him – but I mourned Ginger for years afterwards.

After Pepper died (and I'm sure he *did* go to doggie paradise where he and Ginger play to this day), it was a long time between dogs. We moved around a lot and lived in apartments which weren't suitable for pets. It was only after Shirley and I married and had a family that dogs re-entered my life.

First came Nixie, a black lab. Unfortunately, we only had her a short time. I was transferred to England and we had to give her away.

When we returned, we acquired Snoopy, an obnoxious beagle that had been badly treated as a puppy and hated men as a result. A woman friend had obtained her from the pound but couldn't handle her. We agreed to take her in.

At first, it was a disaster. Snoopy was a nervous wreck who relieved herself everywhere, chewed on furniture and shunned human touch. She seemed totally beyond redemption but she was a pretty dog with intelligent eyes so we persevered.

It took several weeks but we gradually won her affection and the kids loved her. She had lots of personality but she was a glutton. One Easter she went through the house and devoured all the chocolate eggs I had hidden for the kids' big egg hunt in the morning, foil wrappers and all. Miraculously, she survived. On another occasion, she polished off a prize salmon Shirley had just baked for guests when we left it unattended in the kitchen for ten minutes. For days afterwards, her stomach looked like that of a boa constrictor that's just swallowed a pig whole.

Like all beagles, she was a roamer, sometimes getting off her chain and disappearing for days at a time. But she always came home.

Shortly after we moved to Toronto, she developed a tumour and had to be put to sleep; we were all miserable.

After Snoopy came Paddy. He was also a pass-along, a Shetland sheepdog some friends had to find a new home for when they moved to Australia. We'd never been around Shelties before and Paddy was a revelation. He was friendly, playful, protective and personable. He didn't run off for days at a time as Snoopy had done and never ate our salmon. When he died of kidney failure at the young age of seven, it was like losing part of the family.

Shirley and I agreed after that we would never get another dog. The kids were grown, we were travelling more, and a dog was just an encumbrance. Plus they were expensive, demanding and they all had bad breath. Who needed it?

Our resolution lasted four weeks. Then Shirley read an

ad for Sheltie puppies. "We'll just go look," she said. That line somehow had a familiar ring.

A week later, we went back to the puppy farm to pick up Misty Blue Shadow – Misha for short. He was a black and white fur ball with stubby legs and a face that would melt a statue's heart. It was the first time in my life we had ever paid for a dog. Five hundred dollars! "He'd better be worth it," I grumbled to Shirley. "He will be," she confidently replied.

Misha was barely a year old when the renovations began. But he quickly became an active, if often unwelcome, participant in the process.

Five of his basic instincts came into play as the work crews began to arrive.

The first was the Sheltie as defender of the hearth. Shelties are extremely protective of their masters, and Misha is no exception. Most dogs bark when someone comes to the house. That's just a warm-up for Misha. Although he weighs only sixteen pounds (most of a Sheltie is thick fur), he hurls himself at the door repeatedly when anyone appears outside, with the apparent ferocity of a wounded lion. I've seen couriers shrink back in stark terror at these assaults.

Of course, as soon as anyone is admitted it becomes apparent it's all show. In fact, the reason for all the histrionics seems to be his excitement at the prospect of welcoming someone new and getting petted for his trouble. But the first tradespeople who arrived to work on the kitchen regarded him with apprehension. One burly six-footer even cowered on the doorstep and refused to enter until we had confined our fierce pet to another part of the house.

The second instinct to come into play was the Sheltie as herder. These dogs were originally bred to herd sheep in the harsh highlands of Scotland. If there are no sheep to herd, they'll herd anything else that's handy.

In an urban environment, that usually means people. For example, Misha herds me to breakfast every morning. While I'm drinking my orange juice and reading the paper, he watches and listens to everything Shirley is doing in the kitchen. The moment the toaster pops up he starts barking at me, insisting I get moving. He's at my heels all the way into the kitchen. When I sit, he bites the rung of the chair – we can only assume that now that the sheep is in the pen, he's closing the gate. Only when I'm settled in will he go to eat his own food.

This herding instinct extended to all the workmen who came through the house. Whenever they moved, Misha was at their heels, helping them along. He doesn't bite anyone, you understand, he just nudges you to keep you moving in the right direction.

This can be kind of cute for a while but Misha carries it to extremes. The simple act of walking downstairs becomes a life-threatening experience when Misha's around. He's deft at staying a few inches away from your feet but I dread the day when he miscalculates on a staircase. Carrying boxes or equipment with a dog dancing around your ankles can be especially hazardous. Clearly, something had to be done.

Shirley responded by building a dog barrier out of an old cardboard box. The idea was to use it as a gate to block off the stairs. We'd keep Misha in the family room, well away from all the activity in the kitchen. The work crews would be safe and our sanity would be preserved.

That's when we became aware of the persistence instinct.

Shelties have a one-track mind. Once they decide on an objective, they will spend hours, even days, working to achieve it. You may distract them temporarily but they'll be back at it again before long.

Misha saw Shirley's cardboard gate as a challenge that had to be overcome. He immediately set about to do exactly that. His first tactic was to whine pitifully. When that brought no response, he switched to a demanding bark. When we still didn't respond, he launched his own attack in almost military fashion.

First, he reconnoitred, carefully examining the cardboard impediment from all angles; then he started to probe for weaknesses, pawing at it and butting it with his nose.

It didn't take him long to discover that a few well-placed butts got the barrier quivering. When that happened, a little daylight would appear at one corner. That prompted the frontal assault. He quickly inserted his paw into the small space and began to pull. Within moments the cardboard gate came tumbling down and he was dashing back up the stairs to continue his herding work.

We tried replacing the cardboard with a heavy wooden board. That's when we discovered Shelties have tremendous power in their back legs. Misha could launch himself from a standing position like a jump-jet. Three-foot-high boards? He scoffed at them.

We tried chairs instead. They must have been twice his height. He cleared them effortlessly.

Finally, we gave up and told the workers they'd have to live with being herded. Fortunately, they by now were so amused at our vain efforts to contain the animal that they accepted this conclusion with good grace.

The fourth Mishian instinct to affect our renovations was his compulsion to chase things. Squirrels, dogs, cats, raccoons, ghosts – Misha chases them.

Since we don't let him out except on a long chain, he chases them in the house. He'll sit for hours staring out a downstairs window. When he sees something that catches his attention, he'll start barking frantically and dash upstairs. There he discovers that he can no longer see whatever it is he's barking at so he dashes downstairs again. This process continues until he exhausts himself or the offending creature has been gone for half an hour.

Naturally, we tend to find this rather a nuisance, especially when one of us is trying to catch a nap. But we didn't realize how hazardous it could be to our possessions until one summer afternoon.

We were having some painting done upstairs. In another futile attempt to keep the dog at bay, the cardboard barrier was back in place.

The painter was working on the living room ceiling,

using a paint tray into which he'd dip his roller every so often. It was a warm, quiet afternoon so he'd opened the door to the deck to keep fresh air circulating through the room.

Misha, as usual, was positioned at the downstairs window, surveying the activities in the ravine. Suddenly, he went into a barking fit – I don't know to this day what set him off.

He turned to dash up the stairs, only to find the cardboard gate blocking his way. Instead of going through the butting and pawing routine, he simply hurled himself at it. It crumpled and he was gone.

The startled painter saw a black and white streak flash by and run straight through the paint tray. From there, finding Misha was no problem. A neat line of white dog tracks extended across the living room rug and out onto the deck, where the dog was scanning the ground below, looking for his imaginary quarry. When we tried to catch him, he immediately sensed he'd done something wrong and deftly darted away – leaving more white paw prints in his wake, of course. By the time we finally captured him the deck floor looked like a wallpaper pattern.

From that day on, the painter kept his tray on a table top.

Misha found other ways to make painters' lives miserable. Of course, he was only trying to help – but a helpful dog is the last thing a painter needs.

Take a simple task like spreading drop sheets. Misha saw it as a great game. A huge white sheet fluttering? Well, of course – grab the end and run with it. We returned home from shopping one morning to find a cursing painter pulling at one end of a drop sheet while a delighted dog tugged happily at the other. At fifty dollars an hour, I figured I'd better find some other way for the painter to occupy his time. Misha was exiled to the back yard.

The fifth instinct was curiosity. Shelties are curious enough to begin with, but Misha has always been in a league of his own. He has to see everything that's going on and sniff anyone who comes in.

Carpenters hold a special intrigue for him. We sometimes think he may have been one in another incarnation. Let a carpenter in the door and Misha is by his side for the day. He'll lie in a Sphinx-like position in dust and dirt for hours alertly watching the man work. Not even loud hammering scares him off.

Fortunately, all the carpenters who helped on our renovations had a sense of humour. How else can you cope with a staring dog?

Misha's fascination had one practical advantage. If a carpenter left a screw or a nail behind, the dog would invariably find it, scoop it up in his mouth, and proudly deposit it at Shirley's feet. He never swallowed one – at least, as far as we know.

His obsession with carpenters only became a problem at clean-up time. All dogs hate vacuum cleaners, I assume because of the sound. But Misha carries this one step farther. He also hates brooms – at least, busy brooms.

As long as a broom isn't doing anything, he ignores it. It can stand in a corner for days, unworthy of his attention. But the moment anyone starts to sweep, he attacks. No active broom straw is safe in his presence. He snaps and snarls to the point where, if a broom had consciousness, it would have a nervous breakdown.

Carpenters use brooms a lot. They sweep up shavings and sandings and cuttings and lots more. But it reached the point when they were reluctant to clean up at the end of the day. Misha's anti-broom fury unnerved them. We finally had to reach a compromise – when it came time to clean up, I had to take Misha for his evening walk. I know he suspected what was going on but no self-respecting dog will pass up a walk for anything – not even to bark at brooms. In the hierarchy of a dog's life, checking out scatological reference points ranks even higher than harassing carpenters.

Somehow, through all this, the renovations got done. I'm sure to this day Misha believes he played an important part in making it all happen. I still come across him at times, staring into an empty kitchen, perhaps thinking of the great carpenters he's known and dreaming of once again confronting flashing brooms.

The Dog's Stamping on the Deck Again

All the houses on our street were built with a tiny rear balcony attached.

I'm not sure what the original contractor had in mind but I suspect it was simply a marketing ploy. "Magnificent deck overlooking treed ravine." It would add thousands of dollars to the asking price of the house.

Whatever the motive, the houses were blessed with these postage-stamp appendages, which were barely large enough for two chairs and a barbecue. The construction was so rickety that whenever one of our dogs walked across it, the whole deck vibrated. Since the largest dog we ever owned in this house weighed no more than twenty-five pounds, you can appreciate my apprehension whenever I was called upon to perform barbecue duty. You can also understand why we never, ever spent any time out there.

It was on one of my infrequent visits to the barbecue that I discovered we had a more serious problem than I had first realized. That was when I put my hand on the balcony railing, and came away with a big chunk of it. By now I was well aware that the porch was of substandard construction but, even so, this seemed a bit much.

Curiously, I inspected the chunk of wood I was holding. As I did so, I noticed a very large, agitated black ant crawling up my arm. I looked at the piece of railing again. Dozens of its cousins were emerging from holes in the wood, angry at having their meal disturbed.

I dropped the ant farm and fled.

The next day the exterminator arrived.

"Yep," he drawled. "Sure are carpenter ants. Seen lots of them around this year."

Could he get rid of them?

"Easy. But I can't promise they won't come back. And I can't do nothing about all those tunnels they've dug in your wood. Ask me, the whole balcony's probably rotten by now. That's the way these guys work. You don't know you got a problem till the deck falls down."

We consulted. Our long-term plans *did* call for a new back deck. But that was well down the road, after bathrooms, the family room, new carpeting, living room furniture, a new bed and a redesigned office for me.

"What happens if we don't do anything for a while?"

"Well, those critters will just keep chomping away. Let's put it this way – if I was you, I sure wouldn't stand underneath this thing for very long."

There comes a time when long-range plans have to give way to expediency. This was one of those moments.

"Get rid of the ants," I instructed. "We'll take it from there."

Ever since we'd moved into the house, we'd always felt vaguely guilty about not using our back area. One of the reasons we'd bought the place originally was because of the ravine. We couldn't afford a cottage but this would almost be like country living right in the heart of the city just a stone's throw from highway 401.

The ravine certainly had its attractions: mature weeping willows, some towering white birches, red maples, beeches, oaks, with a few flowering trees of indeterminate species tossed in for good measure.

All that foliage is a haven for birds. In the winter, we could teach the kids to recognize chickadees, blue jays, cardinals, redpolls, finches and assorted varieties of wood-peckers. Summer brought robins, orioles, flickers, mourning doves and the occasional grosbeak.

Plus there was the usual city animal life: raccoons, groundhogs (of which more later), squirrels, rabbits, foxes and some very unwelcome skunks. Generally, but not always, we managed to co-exist peacefully.

Nature at our doorstep. Wonderful – except that we never used it. The trembling balcony, combined with dark, overhanging trees and mosquitoes that made even the car-penter ants look small, turned our back yard into a kind of no-go zone. Oh, the kids played there occasionally when they were younger – but you may have noticed that kids are always drawn to places their parents won't go near.

Now it was time to change all that.

We called in Bob, a local handyman a friend had recom-mended. He surveyed the situation and came up with a sketch for a new deck. When I saw it, I thought he'd mixed up our plan with an observation platform for an African game park.

His idea was to build a deck that extended the full length of our back yard almost to the wood lot line. That would make it just about as long as the house itself! Naturally, Bob's cost estimate reflected this ambitious scheme. We thanked him for his time and phoned someone else.

Rod turned out to be one of those consummate professionals you feel comfortable with from the first meeting. He was a no-nonsense guy who'd been building decks for years. He was honest, candid and reliable. When you find someone like this in the building trades, you grab on to him like a leech.

From the outset, he made one thing clear – he would not work with pressure-treated wood. It had an unattractive greenish tinge and didn't stain well. He also considered it dangerous to his workers because of the chemicals used to preserve it. (One of them is arsenic. If you ever work with pressure-treated wood, be sure to wear gloves.)

Rod used natural British Columbia red cedar only. It was more expensive but that was how it was. If we didn't like the idea, he'd be pleased to recommend someone else. We agreed red cedar would be just fine.

Rod was a builder. He was not, however, an innovative designer, as he was the first to admit. He could follow blueprints just fine but someone else had to supply the imagination.

We'd decided after our experience with Bob that we didn't want just an ordinary deck. No rectangular boxes here; if we were going to do it, it would be done right. I wanted a first-class design that would add to the value of our home.

"What you need is a landscape architect," Rod said. "I know just the person and she's not expensive. Maybe five hundred."

Joanne arrived, took numerous photos, and tut-tutted over the fragile condition of the balcony we'd inherited. (We sent Misha out to walk on it for her benefit; the porch shook but remained standing.) In the meantime, I'd been doodling some ideas about what the deck might look like. I have no artistic talent so I had no business making suggestions to a professional but heck – I was paying the bill. I pushed my doodles across the table.

"Maybe something with a hexagonal shape," I said. "Just not a rectangle, please. And some protection from the sun would be nice."

She glanced at my scribbles, tossed them into her file folder and left. A week later she was back. We sat at the dining room table and she spread an artist's rendition before us. We gasped.

Joanne had taken my simple hexagon design and transformed it into a two-pod deck. The larger pod extended out fourteen feet from the house and was twenty-two feet long. It would serve for barbecuing and outdoor dining and would be open to the sky. It would contain a built-in storage cabinet which would double as a server base for open-air meals.

The smaller pod extended out eleven feet and was twelve feet wide. Five inches lower – one step – it was to be topped by a wooden trellis which would produce ever-changing sun and shade patterns over the course of a day. It would be used as a cosy sitting area for reading, conversations or just enjoying nature.

At each end of the deck there would be a decorative lattice privacy screen. We have great neighbours but no one wants people peering at them while they eat.

Below, on the ground level, a second deck to be built with exactly the same proportions, had one major difference. The large pod had provision for a hot tub to be built into the centre of it. A hot tub! Warm, swirling water to ease aching muscles after a long day. What a terrific idea!

I had nothing but praise for Joanne. She'd not only come up with a unique plan (we'd seen nothing like it in all the deck books we'd studied) but she'd also incorporated my ideas into it. In a way, it was *my* deck. She was terrific, wonderful, a genius . . .

Then I got her bill. It was more than double what I expected. She was a thief, a con-woman, a . . .

"She's created something that will be envied by everyone who sees it," Shirley sweetly reminded me. "You're going to bitch over a few hundred extra dollars for a work of art?"

I shut up and wrote the cheque.

Rod's crew arrived in the middle of the most prolonged heat wave we'd experienced in years.

There were two of them – Sean and William. They became part of our lives for the next two months, so we got to know them well.

Sean was an Ulsterman. He wasn't much to look at – short, prematurely greying, with thick bottle-bottom glasses. But personable! He was the incarnation of the Irishman who could charm birds out of the trees.

"You'll find he never brings a lunch," Rod had told us. "The ladies always take care of him."

Shirley was no exception. The day after they arrived, a cooler full of soft drinks had taken a permanent station just inside the back door.

"It's ninety degrees out there and seventy in here," she explained. "I feel guilty."

"For heaven's sake, they're used to it."

"That doesn't make it any cooler."

Shirley made it her business to see that Sean and William were properly looked after. There was coffee in the morning, cold beer at the end of a long Saturday, snacks and sandwiches through the day. No work crew ever had things so good.

"Aren't we paying enough for this contract?" I grumbled as Shirley took down another plate of goodies.

"Do you want them to do a decent job or not? Consider it an investment," she replied.

Like many Irishmen, Sean was skilled at his work but dissatisfied with his lot in life. He was a man with a dream – to become a millionaire by age thirty-five. In an attempt to achieve this goal, he invested much of what he earned in penny stocks trading on the Vancouver Exchange. Most of them plummeted. I suggested one day he would be better off buying lottery tickets but he said he didn't like the odds.

He worked long, hard hours and was very good at his trade. But at night he went into a phone booth and changed into a different person. He played drums in a band at a downtown bar and gunned around the city in an old Porsche. I never figured out where he got all the energy after working on our deck twelve hours a day.

Women apparently flocked to him, attracted by his amiable wit and sturdy physique. But, as far as we could tell, he was a confirmed bachelor. One colleen he had known in Ireland gave up everything back home and came to Toronto to be with him. She moved in and for the next several months cooked his food, washed his clothes, cleaned his apartment and, presumably, shared his bed. If all this was in the hope that he would cave in and marry her, she must have been deeply disappointed. Her visitor's visa expired and she returned home, still single.

His workmate, William, was a completely different type. He was from one of the islands, Barbados we suspected, although he was always somewhat vague about it. Perhaps that was because rumour had it there was a wife and children back home – as well as the wife and children in Toronto.

Whatever the truth, William was soft-spoken, polite, accommodating and hard-working. He lacked Sean's aggressive extroversion but he could be charming too in his own quiet way.

Together, they made an efficient team.

They had to be. The task they were undertaking wasn't easy.

Joanne's elaborate blueprint involved some highly skilled carpentry. The smaller pod was to be cantilevered – a somewhat tricky procedure, I was led to understand. Building the deck on two levels was another difficult challenge. We had declined to purchase prefabricated latticework for the privacy screens – it looked too cheap, we decided – so that had to be constructed from scratch. To top it all off, it turned out our house was built on a slight slope, so the deck had to be built the same way to avoid creating a jackknifed look. One thing about our renovations – they always presented a challenge.

Taking down the old balcony was easy. They removed

the two support posts, gave it a couple of nudges with a crowbar, and it fell down by itself. My nervousness about letting the dog onto it had been vindicated.

As soon as the balcony came down, we experienced a strange phenomenon in our downstairs family room. Light. The sun actually shone in the windows. We were entranced.

"Maybe we shouldn't build an upper deck at all," I said to Shirley. "This room has never looked so good."

"If we don't, we're going to have a sliding door to nowhere upstairs," she observed dryly. "Somebody's going to walk out of it someday and find themselves standing in space. Maybe one of our kids."

"No one would be that stupid," I replied. Actually, I wasn't really sure. People do strange things at parties.

We went out to discuss it with Sean. Well, we didn't *really* discuss it with him – we just argued the question back and forth in front of him while he drummed his fingers on a cedar post.

When we finished, we looked at him expectantly for an adjudication. But Sean was too smooth for that.

"Well, Mr. Pape, I can certainly see your point. A nice, bright family room with no overhang would be glorious. But Mrs. Pape's right about that sliding door. You'd have to replace it – I'd guess that would cost, oh, maybe fifteen hundred dollars. Then there's all this wood we've got piled back here. We'd have to send it back. Rod can tell you what that would cost but I'd say a few hundred anyway. Then there's those drawings you paid so much for. And of course you realize you're paying for my time – William's too – while we're standing here. But if you want to take more time to think about it . . ."

I know when I'm beaten. The work began.

The first task was to erect the support posts. There were five of them, huge, six-inch square cedar beams. Two – the ones that would support the trellis over the small pod – were twenty feet in length; the rest were twelve feet.

Sean and William had to dig the four-foot deep post holes by hand, since there wasn't enough space to manoeuvre a digging machine into the back yard. The posts were then set in, aligned, creosoted and encased in concrete.

I didn't pay much attention to the procedure until I glanced out of the window at the end of the day.

"Haven't they put in a short post where one of the tall ones should be?" I asked Shirley.

"I'm sure they wouldn't make a simple mistake like that," she said. "They know how to read blueprints."

"Haven't you put in a short post where one of the tall ones should be?" I asked Sean when they arrived the next day.

He took one look. The Irish are noted for their colourful use of oaths. I was treated to the full spectrum in the minutes that followed.

That was the only major hitch, however. After that, things proceeded relatively smoothly.

Oh, Misha didn't like the sound of bolts being rivetted into the side of the house and spent the whole day barking at the offending noise which, of course, only compounded the racket.

And what little grass there was out back didn't like having lumber piled on it and promptly punished us by turning yellow.

But as the deck took shape and we saw how handsome it was going to be, these aggravations seemed trivial.

"How wide apart do you want the posts in the railing?" Sean asked one day as the work neared completion.

"Just wide enough so the dog can't get through," Shirley said.

I had difficulty imagining Misha leaping off a second-storey deck in pursuit of a squirrel but I kept quiet. If we made the spacing larger and he ever did such a crazy thing, it would be my fault.

The final stage was for William to build the cedar cabinet to house our barbecue utensils, outdoor dishes and other deck paraphernalia. We'd thought about adding other built-ins, including two cedar benches, but Rod had steered us away from the idea even though it would have meant extra business for him.

"The deck may look huge on paper but as soon as you start putting furniture out there it's going to shrink," he said. "You can always add benches later if you want."

So we settled on just the cabinet.

William did a fine job. The cabinet turned out to be the perfect finishing touch to the deck. It was only afterwards he told us he'd never built anything like it before. Talk about learning on the job!

On the last day, we had a little farewell party for Sean and William. We took out a bottle of sparkling wine and we all toasted the deck; then Shirley presented them with some trout we'd caught along with a bottle of white wine each to go with the fish. William also got a bottle of good rum, while Sean received a bottle of Jameson's. I wondered if he *ever* had to buy his own food or booze.

When they were gone, we surveyed our new outdoor domain. The cedar seemed to glow in the late afternoon sun. The new Samsonite furniture looked cool and inviting. The hanging baskets of flowers that Shirley had strategically positioned around the deck added colour and vibrancy to the picture.

We invited Misha to come out. He dashed across the floor to the railing and peered down at the lawn. The deck didn't quiver.

He spotted a cat in a neighbouring yard and began yelping. The railings contained him. He did not hurl himself into space – although I suspect he would have done so if he could. I silently blessed Shirley's intuition.

I lit the barbecue and tossed on a couple of steaks. It was a moment to savour. We did.

Why Is My Hair Freezing?

There was just one problem with our new decks. The bottom one had a big hole in the middle of it.

It was there for a reason, of course. That's where the hot tub would be, if we could ever find someone to take it out of the garage and install it.

We had originally discussed the idea of putting a swimming pool into the back yard. That conversation lasted, oh, maybe three minutes.

We'd already had an experience with a swimming pool, you see. Only a masochist would go through that a second time.

The pool came with the first house we ever owned in Ottawa. When we viewed the property on a hot July day it looked like a back yard paradise. We pictured ourselves sipping gin and tonic under a patio umbrella, soaking up rays, and slipping into the crystal clear water periodically to cool off. What a life! We bought the place largely on the strength of that vision.

We did have days like that – a few of them. But we paid heavily for them.

Summer is short in central Canada. Even with a heater, the pool season at best runs from mid-May to mid-September. For the other eight months of the year our back yard was dominated by a stagnant death trap.

The first official sign that the swimming season was winding down was the worms.

"There's something strange about the bottom of the pool," Shirley said. This was near the end of our first summer in the house.

I went out back and looked. There was indeed something strange. The bottom of the pool was littered with – what? Dirt? Leaves? But they hadn't started to fall yet. Anyway, the only trees in close proximity were conifers.

I grabbed the skimmer net and probed. When I brought it to the surface, it was full of dead worms. Yuk!

"I'm not going back in there until you clean out every one of them," Shirley said. I spent the next two hours doing exactly that.

The next morning the pool floor was again covered with dead worms. I again cleaned them out.

The next day there were more. And the next. And the next.

"What the hell is going on?" I muttered as I scooped up

yet another netful of worm carcasses.

We consulted our pool man.

"It's your pool heater."

"What?"

"Yeah. It's starting to get cold at night. The warm water attracts the worms. They fall in and drown."

I had a mental picture of hundreds of worms slithering across our patio in the dead of night in search of a warm place to bed down. I decided against doing any star-gazing for a while.

"What can we do about it?"

"Turn off the heater."

"But then the water will get cold."

"That's right. So the worms won't be drawn to it."

"But then we won't be able to swim."

He shrugged as if to say: "Hey, I solved your problem. What more do you want?"

Autumn worms were only one of the hazards of owning a pool in a cold climate. When the season ended, it had to be winterized. Since this was an old-fashioned fibreglass pool, it couldn't be drained, however.

"Got to keep the water in all year round," the pool man said. "Equalizes the pressure on the pool walls. Otherwise the freezing of the ground in winter will crack them like egg shells."

But what about ice build-up in the pool? Wouldn't that do the same thing?

"Sure. That's why you have to put in logs every fall. They absorb the ice pressure. We do it all for you. It'll cost you. . ."

During the winter the pool became part of the back yard snowscape. Our first near-disaster occurred as spring approached.

Our black Labrador, Nixie, had become used to romping in the fenced-in yard over the winter. But one day in late March she started trotting across the pool ice to her favourite squat-spot – and promptly plunged through. Crisis time! The family dog was struggling in frigid water, out of our reach. The ice was clearly too dangerous to step on to try to reach her.

Throwing a life preserver didn't seem like an appropriate response, even if we'd had one handy.

So we did what any quick-thinking person would do in that situation – we raced up and down the side of the pool yelling meaningless orders at her.

Fortunately, she ignored us. After the initial shock, she assessed the situation and started paddling towards the closest side. When she reached ice, she put her two front paws up, broke through it, and paddled on. She finally got close enough for us to reach her and pull her out. Our reward was a cold shower as she shook herself. We were shivering when we went inside. Nixie was fine.

The second near-disaster happened a month later. Kimberley was two at the time and followed her mother around like a tiny shadow. As a precaution, Shirley had rigged up a harness with an empty Javex bottle tied to the back which she slipped onto Kim whenever they were around the pool. It made the poor little tyke look ridiculous but as Shirley reminded me when I said something disparaging: "Nixie could swim. Kim can't."

Sure enough, one day in late April when Shirley was cleaning up in the pool area, Kim strayed too close to the edge and fell in. Thank heaven, the Javex bottle brought her bobbing back to the surface immediately and all Shirley had to do was reach down and pluck her out. We owe an eternal debt of thanks to Colgate-Palmolive, who make the product.

We sold the Ottawa house a year later.

"No more pools, okay?" Shirley said on the day we moved out.

"No more pools," I promised.

Which is why we compromised on a hot tub.

Joanne had incorporated one into her deck drawings. We loved the idea. Warm, swirling waters at the end of a long, hard day. What better way to sooth tired muscles and ease away tension? And the hot tub season was much longer. In fact, we could keep it going all through the winter if we wanted to.

"It's terrific in January," a hot tub salesman assured us. "You just step out your back door and into one hundred degree water. You can get out, roll in the snow, and then get back in. It's exhilarating. I guarantee you've never experienced anything like it."

I wasn't at all sure about the roll in the snow part but the rest seemed pretty enticing. A hot tub it would be.

We went to the Toronto Home Show where we quickly learned that what we wanted wasn't really a hot tub at all. That's the barrel-shaped cedar version they use in California. What we wanted was a spa, made from moulded acrylic. Much more suitable for our climate. And doesn't grow slime on the sides. That was the part that convinced Shirley.

We soon discovered that spas come in all sizes and styles. Making a selection wasn't easy.

You have to decide how many people you want to cram in, how deep you want the water to be, and what kind of seating arrangement you like. You have to think about jets and bubblers and heaters. You need to consider colour, shape and style. Plus there are some incidental matters like price and service.

We went around the city taking off our shoes and lying on our backs in showroom models. We watched in amazement as an elderly saleslady crawled into one with us and proceeded to jump up and down on the seats to demonstrate the spa's strength. She looked like a bouncing elf.

We received conflicting advice from sales people on everything from the size of heater to the best water purification system. The more we learned, the more confused we became.

I started reading books on spas. They confused me even more. By the time I'd read chapters on hydrojets, pumps, filter capacity, heaters, sterilizers, drains and skimmer baskets, most of the magic was gone.

But there was still that hole in the deck. We pushed ahead.

At one point, Shirley was convinced that what she really wanted was a gigantic tub that would easily accommodate a dozen people plus their rubber duckies if they wanted to bring them along.

"I thought you said no more pools," I reminded her.

"But it's on sale," she protested.

"It's still twice as much as anything else we've looked at. And it'll cost twice as much to heat."

"But . . ."

"Plus anything that big is more likely to attract worms." I won that round.

One thing we determined was that a bubbler wasn't such a good idea. A bubbler is one of the many add-ons you can buy that drive spa prices into the stratosphere. Its purpose is, as you might guess, to make more bubbles.

This effect is achieved by drilling a series of small holes in the seats between the inner and outer layers of the acrylic shell. Air is then pumped through these holes to create more bubbling action when the tub is activated.

A friend who already had a spa assured us the effect was most pleasurable. What he didn't realize was that our spa was going to be outside. His was in the house.

"Where do you think the air that creates the bubbles is coming from?" one salesman asked when we inquired about the idea.

Frankly, that hadn't occurred to me.

"It comes from all around you. From the outside atmosphere. So what do you think happens on a winter day? You end up with a damn cold bottom, that's what. And what do you think happens to the water temperature when you pump that freezing air through it?"

I got the picture. No bubbler.

We finally located the spa we liked at a small manufacturer just outside the city. There was no showroom; we just went to the factory, sat in the dusty tub, and decided it fit.

Fit is important in selecting a spa. The seats and the recliners should mould comfortably to your body. If they don't, move on.

The spa had been delivered before the deck was built so that Sean and William could measure it and be sure the hole they left was the right size. Now it was time to make it operational.

Except we couldn't get hold of Steve, the spa company manager. We'd call and leave messages. He didn't return them. We spoke to his assistant. She promised to page him. He didn't call. Days passed. The spa sat in the garage. We had visions of unwelcome animals plunging into the hole in the deck. The ravine had more than its share of skunks.

"I told you we shouldn't have paid him until it was installed," Shirley said.

I nodded glumly.

Then he called.

"When's your crew coming?" I asked eagerly.

"Well, I'm not quite sure. They're pretty busy right now," Steve said guardedly.

"When will they be unbusy?"

"Ah, Mr. Pape, you realize of course that the price you paid didn't include installation?"

"It didn't?"

"No, sir."

"Did you think I planned to keep it sitting in my garage?"

"Well, sir, some people like to install the spa themselves."

"I don't think I'm quite up to that. How much is installation?"

"I'd say about a thousand."

"When can your crew be here?"

"Saturday morning. Nine a.m."

The "crew" was Steve and a buddy.

"I thought you were the manager," I said to him.

"Well, yeah, but I kinda like to keep on top of all parts of the business."

"This operation is even smaller than I thought," I said to Shirley when I went inside.

Finally, they got it set up and running. It looked great. I couldn't wait to get in.

"There's a few more things you'll need," Steve said as he

packed up his tools.

"Such as?"

"Well, you'll want a water-testing kit." He pulled one from the back of his truck. "Don't want to let the pH get too high. Makes a real smell. You can even get calcium scale on the walls."

"Sure don't want that," I murmured.

"If the pH gets too high, add some muriatic acid. Here's a bottle of that. If the water gets too acidic, put in some of this alkaline solution." He produced another big bottle.

"You'll also want some water clarifier." Another big bottle.

"And I strongly recommend this Bubble Away." Yet another big bottle.

"What's that for?" I asked.

"You'll see. And, oh yeah, chlorine." A huge bucket.

"Wait a minute. I thought that expensive ozonator we bought was all we need to purify the water."

I knew all about ozonators, or ozone generators, from my reading. They feed a steady stream of ozone gas into the water that breaks down organic chemicals into carbon dioxide and water. An efficient one should do a complete sterilization job or so I thought.

"Well, it's *almost* all you need. But to be on the safe side, we do recommend tossing in a couple of scoops of chlorine every so often."

"How often?"

"Oh, just a couple of times a day. Now let's see, that all comes to. . ."

"Don't ask," I said to Shirley as I walked back into the house with my arms full of bottles. "At least it's running."

We got into our bathing suits and luxuriated in it. It was everything we'd imagined.

"This is the life," I remarked, as we sat up to our necks in the warm, coursing water.

All the problems were behind us. Now we could just relax and enjoy.

From the beginning, we were conscious of the importance of maintaining healthy water.

"Too many people end up sitting in their own dirt," one spa owner said to us, wrinkling her nose. "You've got to make sure the water is always clean. Otherwise, you can get all kinds of diseases, like . . ."

I didn't need to hear more. Our spa would be hygienically pure.

"I don't understand this," I said to Shirley a few days later.

"What?"

"This is the fourth time I've tested the water today. First, the pH was too acid, so I put in some alkaline solution; then it was too alkaline, so I added some muriatic acid; then . . . well, I can't seem to get it right."

"You're probably putting in too much each time. Let me do it."

She experimented some more, adding a drop of this and two drops of that. Finally, the pH tester was satisfied. I crawled into the tub and turned on the jets.

The first indication I had that something was wrong was a scum on the surface of the water. That quickly turned into small bubbles which rapidly became large bubbles.

I got out of the tub.

"You'd better come look at this," I shouted upstairs to Shirley.

By the time we got back, the spa looked as if it had been overdosed with washing soap. Mountains of grey-scummed bubbles rose from the surface.

"Maybe this is what that Bubble Away is for." Shirley said.

We poured some in. The bubbles subsided, but the scum remained.

"I don't think I'll go back in today," I said.

"Good thinking," Shirley said. "You'd probably dissolve."

I took a sample of our spa water to a local pool supplies store to be analyzed.

"How long has this water been in there?" the sales clerk asked when he gave me the results.

"About three days."

He looked at me in disbelief.

"Well, you'd better get rid of it. What you've got there isn't really water at all. It's some kind of chemical stew. I sure wouldn't set foot in it."

After that, I stopped worrying about pH balance. I toss in some chlorine occasionally and check to see that the water looks clear. If any bacteria did dare to venture in, I figure that between the ozonator and the chlorine, we'll get them.

The spa proved to be a great hit with our children, especially our son, who took to romancing his various girl-friends in it. The problem was he chose the middle of the night for this activity. After a couple of weeks of waking up to gushing waters and soft murmuring beneath our bedroom window, we placed a curfew on spa activities. Our children are of age and can conduct their love lives as they wish – so long as they don't keep us awake in the process.

That didn't deter Kendrew from using the spa, however. He just changed tactics. It became an excuse for a party.

First, there was a tub-warming party; then a graduation breakfast party; then he invited a few dozen of his fellow lifeguards over to try it out. A record twenty-one of them crammed in at once, half emptying the water. One was kind enough to deposit a wad of green bubble gum on a seat. The back deck resembled a bomb site when they all left.

We issued a cease and desist order on spa parties. Kendrew couldn't understand what we were upset about.

Autumn came and we kept the hot tub going. Watching the trees change colour while warm water swirled around me was a unique experience.

Winter arrived and the hot tub bubbled on. We kept the water at a constant ninety-eight degrees (the perfect tempera-ture for a spa; anything hotter can raise body heat to some-times dangerous levels). So there was no danger of a freeze-up.

I had pictured myself sitting in the tub, watching the first snowfall of the season with hot stream rising all around me. Just like in Banff.

What I didn't realize was that, while the water may be ninety-eight, the air is seventy degrees colder. And, unless you're wearing scuba gear, your head is in the air.

The first winter day I was in the spa, I experienced a most uncomfortable sensation. My body was luxuriously warm. But I kept feeling rivulets of icy water on the back of my neck.

"No wonder," Shirley said when she came out to see what was happening. "Your hair is frozen in the back. In fact, I can even see little icicles."

I curtailed my winter spa activities after that. But Kendrew thought it was great and kept inviting friends over. It was mid-January and we had young people in bathing suits running in and out of our family room.

"We don't need to go to Florida for spring break this year," one of them remarked while passing through. "We've got your place."

I smiled weakly.

Then the electricity bill arrived.

"There has to be some mistake," I said to Shirley. "This is about triple what we normally pay."

"I agree it seems strange," the woman at Ontario Hydro said when I called. "Have you had any changes in your pattern of electricity use? Any new appliances or heating devices?"

"No, nothing except. . ."

We decided to close down the spa for the winter. Kendrew was devastated. I guess his friends were too, since they were now doomed to Florida.

"Nobody ever said the electric bill would be so high," I complained to Shirley.

"No one ever said a lot of things about spas," she observed.

I know one couple who had so much trouble with their hot tub they finally filled it in. We haven't taken such drastic action. Oh sure, there have been other problems since and it's an expensive toy. But to lie back at the end of the day and just let go while the warm water massages your aching body – well, some pleasures are worth the trouble that comes with them.

And, no – we've never found a worm in it.

What Do You Do With a Pregnant Groundhog?

For years the green space behind our house – I hesitate to dignify it with the word lawn, much less garden – was largely neglected.

The dominant impression when we walked out the back door was of trees closing in from all directions.

To the left were two hawthorns, one male, one female. Not that I could tell the difference, of course. An arborist informed us they were of the opposite sex. I have to admit we never observed any untoward activity between them.

If you've ever lived in close proximity to these trees, you'll know they have four characteristics:

1) A magnificent display of white flowers every spring (which lasts about two days).

2) Needle-like thorns that can pierce a bare foot or put out an eye in an instant.

3) Vulnerability to a fungus that produces unsightly rust-coloured spots on the leaves for most of the summer.

4) An autumn fruit crop that attracts every squirrel within a five-mile radius and litters the ground with squishy red berries that kids delight in tromping on just before they come in for dinner.

In short, the price of two days of spring beauty is a summer of unsightliness, an autumn of stained carpeting, and a constant risk to life and limb.

My wife perceived this was a bad trade-off within a couple of years of moving in; however, staunch defender of the rights of trees that I am, I refused to do anything about it. Cut down a tree? Never!

The hawthorns weren't the only beneficiaries of this environmentalist phase I was going through. The jungle directly behind the house also thrived as a result – to the point where the back yard became so dark from overhanging limbs that about all that would grow was a healthy crop of toad-stools.

It was our next door neighbours who finally forced the issue. One of the hawthorn trees was on their property. We came back from a weekend trip one May to find it gone!

At first, I was incensed; then Shirley pointed out that we were suddenly getting some sunlight in our living room and that we could actually see for the first time the magnificent willow trees farther down the ravine.

As the leaves on the remaining hawthorn started turning their annual shade of rust, I conceded that maybe the disappearance of the second tree wouldn't be such a bad thing after all.

Within two days it was gone. My wife wasn't taking any chances I might change my mind.

Suddenly, a whole corner of our yard was bright and sunny, and we could actually see the sky from our back deck.

Wouldn't it be nice, Shirley suggested mildly, if we carried this on a little further? We could trim back those overhanging branches, cut down a few junk trees and – who knows? – something might even start to grow out there. Like grass.

We did. It did. I couldn't believe the transformation. We actually developed a real lawn where once only fungus had flourished.

But that was just the beginning. Having cut back the trees and let in the sun, Shirley decided we should have a real garden. Flowers and all that stuff.

We tried putting in a few plants ourselves with the idea of creating a graceful transition zone from the wild look of the ravine to the placid calm of a genuine lawn.

But nothing seemed to work. Most of the flowers we planted didn't bloom, while the ones that did looked scrawny and out-of-place.

So we decided to consult a landscaper.

The first ones we tried were a young European couple. They looked at the site, went away, and came back with a proposal that included fish ponds, bubbling fountains and statuary.

As they explained their plans in enthusiastic detail, I felt it all seemed a little too ambitious for our modest space.

I knew I was right when they came to the price tag. A thirty-five thousand dollar garden was not what I had in mind.

Next, we consulted a local garden centre that promoted free landscape designs, as long as you bought all the plants from them. When their plans came back, they had plunked a giant blue spruce right in the middle of the lawn and added a couple of birches for good measure.

Just what we needed – more trees.

At this point, we didn't know where to turn; then we attended a party at the home of some friends.

The landscaping around their pool was magnificent – lots of variety without ostentation. It turned out the work had been done by the son-in-law of another couple we knew well.

We called him the next day – his name was Jim. Predictably, he was extremely busy. But eventually we got some of his time.

He produced a design that fitted our needs perfectly. His only recommended change in the natural terrain was to bring in several large rocks that would enable him to create two tiers of plantings and smooth the transition from forest to garden.

The rest of the effect was to be created with the plants themselves. Rustic species, like hemlock, dogwood, and witch hazel, would be set in immediate proximity to the wood lot. Adjacent to the lawn banks of day lilies, two clusters of iris and weigela bushes flanked a small serviceberry tree was the central focus (no thorns, no rust, we were assured).

Close to the house the plan showed cedar-lined pathways bordered with elegant perennials like rhododendrons, dwarf lilacs, hostas and astilbes.

The price was about fifteen thousand dollars. Much of that was for the rocks. I bristled at the notion of paying hundreds of dollars for rocks, but Shirley shushed me.

We told Jim to go ahead.

The result was breathtaking. I couldn't believe our ugly duckling of a back yard could be transformed into such a field of beauty.

We revelled in it for one summer. We watched fluttering robins gorge on the serviceberries when they ripened – the tree's branches were too delicate to support squirrels. We gloried in the ever-shifting patterns of colours – the spring crimson of the rhododendrons, the soft fragrance of ivory lilies of the valley, the June purples of the iris, the lacy whites and pinks of the astilbes, the summer oranges and yellows of the day lilies, the autumn rose of the showy sedums.

We agreed it was one of the best investments we had ever made.

Then the groundhog came.

We'd seen groundhogs in the ravine before. Occasionally, they even ventured onto our property to gorge on hawthorn berries or to nibble away on the tender leaves of some plant we were trying to cultivate.

But never anything like this! It was a full-scale assault. Rodent terrorism.

The first sign was a rustling among the witch hazel bushes at the back of the garden. There was no wind so we took a closer look.

A huge groundhog – by far the biggest I had ever seen – was sitting on her hind quarters, munching contently away on the witch hazel leaves. Every so often she reached up with one paw to pull down a branch so she could systematically strip it.

Naturally, we yelled. She threw a contemptuous glance at us and ambled back into the ravine.

The next day she was back. And the next. And the next.

Our expensive witch hazel plants began to look as if they'd been attacked by a swarm of locusts.

In desperation we erected plastic netting around them. That stopped her. So she went after the hostas instead, munching every new shoot that appeared. We put netting around those too. So she turned her attention to a bed of pansies we had planted. We covered those with netting as well.

"You have a lovely garden," complimented an arborist who was spraying our birch trees, "but what's all this green netting?"

He was incredulous when we told him.

By now we had identified our tormentor's hideout. It was in a neighbour's yard, two houses away. We would stand on our deck in frustration, watching the furry garden-wrecker contentedly sunning herself after destroying another hundred dollars worth of plants.

But there was nothing we could do to stop her.

I grew up in the country where we had a simple solution to such problems.

It was called a gun.

I once saw my father, who had fought in the First World War, pick off a leaping red squirrel in mid-air with a twenty-two rifle at a range of more than one hundred feet – and this in twilight conditions, without the aid of a telescopic sight.

That squirrel deserved its fate – it had been rooting around in our attic.

The groundhog deserved similar. Unfortunately, the police take a dim view of citizens firing off potshots at animals, or anything else, in urban areas.

We had to find another way.

Hiring an animal control professional seemed like a logical course. We got on the phone.

Yes, they could do it. Only not right now. This was mating season, you see. Our groundhog was probably pregnant, which would explain why she was so hungry. And pregnant groundhogs are protected by law.

I couldn't believe it. This ravager a protected species? Had the environmentalists gone mad?

That's the way it is, we were told. But after the babies were born and weaned, they'd be glad to come and do the job. The cost would be two hundred dollars. Of course, they couldn't guarantee that another groundhog wouldn't immediately move in and take over the territory. In fact, that was quite likely.

Animal control didn't seem to be the answer. I asked our neighbours if they had any ideas. It turned out they had plenty. Their gardens were being destroyed too.

One suggested flooding the groundhog's burrow. A brilliant idea, I thought. I obtained permission to enter the yard where the critter was holed up, inserted a hose, and turned on the water full force.

I must have poured dozens of gallons of water down that hole. I had occasional guilt flashes of the poor, helpless animal drowning in the unexpected flood; then I remembered what was happening to our expensive garden and kept the water coming.

The next day the groundhog munched through another hosta bed.

Another neighbour said he had some piano wire in his basement. "We could set a noose at the burrow entrance and garrote her when she comes out," he said. I assumed he was putting me on. But maybe he was serious.

The groundhog became the number one topic of conversation on our street. We'd discuss it over the back fence. We'd compare destruction notes when we met neighbours during dog walks.

All these intelligent, well-educated people suddenly were reduced to a single topic of conversation – groundhogs!

Acting on the "know your enemy" theory, I began to do some research on the rodents. The first thing I discovered is that garden books don't recognize them as pests.

I browsed through every book I could find on the subject. There was all kinds of advice on what to do about aphids, grasshoppers, earwigs, cutworms, leaf miners, grubs, spider mites, sowbugs and other assorted nuisances. Nothing on groundhogs.

Shirley called a gardening phone-in show to ask for help. They suggested using a commercial spray designed to repel all kinds of animals from dogs to deer. It was pricey but so was our garden so we invested in it.

The groundhog munched on.

A newspaper article suggested pests could be deterred from eating leaves that were sprayed with a homemade concoction of dishwashing soap, cayenne pepper and chili powder. Shirley dutifully made up the mess and sprayed all the plants with it. That night it rained. When the groundhog arrived the next morning the leaves were fresh, clean and tasty.

Someone suggested that spreading mothballs around would do the trick. Our garden suddenly looked as if it had been hit by a hail storm and smelled like someone's old closet.

The groundhog munched on.

Shirley read another article that said wild animals will avoid anything that carries human scent. The story suggested that anyone having problems with pests could get rid of them by spreading human hair around.

Willing to try anything at this point, she went to the hairdresser, had her hair cut, and then dumbfounded the poor woman by asking to have it doggie bagged.

By that afternoon, the garden was strewn with my wife's hair.

By the following morning, three more hostas had been demolished. So much for that theory.

Shirley heard that animals are often frightened off by motion, so she came up with the idea of setting out children's toy windmills at strategic points in the garden.

They added extra colour but the groundhog ignored them.

Perhaps some aluminum pie plates suspended from tree branches would do the job. At this point, the neighbours began to think we were losing our minds.

The groundhog munched on.

Sound. We'll scare her off with noise. Wind chimes – just the thing.

We still enjoy the melodious tinkles in the evening. But as far as the groundhog was concerned, it was a non-event.

"Maybe it's because the chimes are up in a tree," Shirley suggested. "Too far away to have any effect."

Acting on that theory, she went out and bought a couple of dozen jingle bells and strung them around the perimeter of the garden with fishing line. The groundhog couldn't get at the goodies without jostling the fishing line and setting off the bells. That would certainly frighten it.

No, they certainly did not. Maybe the groundhog thought it was Santa's sleigh. More likely, it didn't think anything. What are few tinkles when lunch awaits?

Our landscaper came by to see how things were going. "My God," he murmured. "What are all those rusty bells doing in your plants?"

Shirley poured out the tale of woe.

"Traps," he said.

"Traps?"

"I'll get you some animal traps. Wire cages, actually. You lure the groundhog in with some lettuce and the door automatically closes behind her."

I suggested that the groundhog was hardly likely to be tempted by a few leaves of withered lettuce with all those juicy hostas around. I also silently wondered what I would do with an outraged groundhog in a wire cage.

We told him we'd be in touch if we wanted the traps.

In the meantime, I found out something about groundhogs from the encyclopaedia. I learned they are also known as woodchucks – why, I'm not sure. I certainly never saw this one chuck any wood.

They're described as a kind of marmot (what the heck is a marmot?) that grow to about two feet in length. The encyclopaedia acknowledged that they are indeed considered pests but only because they destroy farm crops like alfalfa. Gardens apparently don't count.

I also discovered that the living quarters of the burrow are extremely complex with several compartments. The main living area is constructed above the entry tunnel so that rainwater will wash through underneath while a groundhog sits high and dry. Cunning. Not only that, but a typical burrow will have at least one emergency exit, and sometimes two. No wonder the hose had no effect.

The whole neighbourhood continued to suffer. At least the creature was spreading the misery around.

One family, like us, had just put in a new garden of their own. Their youngest son, who was about twenty at the time, had done much of the work. He couldn't believe what was happening to his mother's plants.

One day, when we were discussing possible solutions, he came up with an idea.

"If we can't use a gun, how about a bow and arrow?" he suggested.

"Great idea," I replied. "Who's going to shoot it?" The

only bow and arrow I'd ever used was the kind that come tipped with rubber suction cups. That was when I was ten.

"I've got one. I will."

The next night when I went out to barbecue, I glanced over to their lawn. There, propped up in the garden, was a piece of plywood with a crude groundhog painted on it. The lad was launching arrows at it and, occasionally, hitting the target.

"Attaboy," I shouted encouragingly.

"We'll get her," he called back.

I frankly don't know how the Indians ever survived. In case you've never noticed, archery competitions use stationary targets with a big bull's eye in the middle. Even then they're tough to hit. Bringing down a moving animal with an arrow requires a combination of strength, vision, dexterity, skill and luck that is far beyond the capability of most human beings. If we had to depend on the bow and arrow to put dinner on the table today, we'd all starve.

As far as I know, our neighbour launched only one shot in the direction of the real groundhog. She eluded it with ridiculous ease. Groundhogs may look clumsy but they can move quickly, particularly when their radar senses incoming arrows or other missiles. (I once pitched a barbecue fork at her in frustration. She dodged and stared at me with mild astonishment before returning to her dinner.)

It was back to the drawing board. Only now the problem was compounded. We suddenly had three groundhogs to contend with, not one. Mama had given birth.

"What about poison?" I suggested one day, as we watched mother and her young sunning themselves by the burrow entrance. She had just taken them on their first guided tour of the neighbourhood with special emphasis on the tasty delights to be found in our garden.

"Can't be done," Shirley said. "Too many other animals around. We'd end up poisoning a bunch of dogs and cats."

"No, not that kind of poison. Poison plants. We set out

plants that are poisonous. The groundhogs won't touch them. Or, if they do, they'll die. Either way, we solve the problem."

We started poring through our gardening books, looking for poisonous flowers. Surprisingly, there are all kinds of them.

"Those with potentially fatal or very serious effects are marked with an asterisk," our gardening book said. We paid special attention to those.

Crocus are on the most-dangerous list. So are foxglove, rhododendrons and azalea. Also poisonous, but not quite as deadly, are daffodils, hyacinth, lily-of-the-valley, English ivy and wisteria. Someone also told Shirley that poppies and delphiniums are unpleasant to the taste.

We headed to the garden centre and bought a couple of hundred dollars worth of dangerous plants. Gleefully, we set them out and waited to see what would happen.

The poppies were the first to go. The groundhogs devoured them within two days. If they *did* taste bad, the groundhogs sure didn't show it. And there were no ill effects, as far as we could see.

Next, the delphiniums. The rodents ate the flowers and the leaves, leaving only the bare stems. Afterwards, they basked in the sun. Not even a hiccup. So much for that piece of neighbourly advice.

We had success with the crocus, to the extent it wasn't eaten. But it only flowers for a short time in the spring. Ditto with the hyacinth and the daffodils.

The foxglove survived – it was too potent even for a groundhog, although insects found it quite palatable, judging by all the holes in the leaves. But it's not a particularly attractive plant. You certainly wouldn't want to fill your garden with it. The groundhogs, mother and babies, simply tiptoed around it and went back to munching hostas. They also feasted on something else we had tried planting – pansies. It was only after the bed lay blighted that someone told me that pansies are one of the great delicacies of the flower world.

If poison plants wouldn't do the job, what else could we try?

Smoke bombs, a gardener suggested. Never failed. Make sure the creatures are inside, then block off all exits and drop a couple of the bombs into the hole. Asphyxiation, quick and deadly. Just don't let any fanatical animal lovers see you do it.

I paid a visit to the hardware store. Yes, they carried them. I took home two packages of four bombs each. This time it was going to be done right.

By now I knew where all the entrances to the burrow were located. I again obtained permission from the neighbours in whose yard the groundhog family resided and sealed off the emergency exits one afternoon when I was sure the animals were inside; then I lit two smoke bombs and tossed them in. I covered the top of the hole with a large rock and waited.

Smoke filtered out from under the rock for some time. There was no sound from beneath the earth. I left the rock in place and went home.

We watched the burrow entrance from our deck for several days. No sign. The plants showed no indication of fresh nibbles.

We began to think we had actually won; then one morning Shirley went out to find mother and babies sunning themselves comfortably beside the big stone. They'd simply dug a new entrance right beside it.

The war was still on!

Desperation was taking hold.

I read that a certain type of terrier can be trained to go right down into holes and kill burrowing animals. But they cost several hundred dollars, plus the training. On top of that, we already had a dog.

I thought about spreading mousetraps all through the garden. They wouldn't kill the beasts but they would at least give them a scare. I actually went out and bought half a dozen traps but then decided against the idea at the last minute. A groundhog limping around the neighbourhood with a mouse-trap dangling from one paw seemed too cruel a punishment even given the heinous crimes they had committed. The traps are still in our basement.

At this point, we were just about at our wit's end. The groundhogs appeared to be here to stay.

And then a very simple idea occurred to me. Why I hadn't thought of it before, I have no idea; it seemed so obvious.

Mrs. Groundhog had created an elaborate network of tunnels and burrows. Even if we got rid of her and the kids, someone else would just move in.

The key, therefore, was not to eliminate the groundhogs; it was to eliminate their home, so they'd decamp somewhere else. True, someone else's garden would become the new dining spot. But that would be their problem. We'd given enough.

I went back to the neighbours whose back yard harboured the main entrance. As soon as I explained the idea, they embraced it enthusiastically. Within days there was a concrete mixer in their yard and a workman was pouring yards of cement down the hole.

I assume the ground hog family escaped by a back door but maybe they didn't. Perhaps they're entombed down there. Frankly, I don't care. The point is, it worked! To this day we've been groundhog free! The plague has been lifted.

There's an epilogue to this story. One June day a couple of years later, Misha and I were out on our daily walk in the woods. We came across two tiny groundhogs, no more than a week or so old, in the middle of the path. The mother was no where in sight.

My immediate inclination was to stomp on them – after all, they would just grow up to be someone else's problem. But then Misha and one of the babies touched noses. The young one showed no fear of the much bigger dog; just curiosity.

How could I do it in after that?

The ceremonial exchange of sniffs ended. Misha looked

back at me, then trotted down the path. I followed, leaving the young groundhogs behind.

I guess I'm not as callous as I thought. They'd just better not show up in our garden one day.

The Designer Knows Best
(Sometimes)

I imposed very few conditions on Shirley's renovations. But there was one on which I was adamant – she had to bring in a professional interior designer to create a master plan for the house.

She wasn't thrilled with the idea at first.

"I can do all that. Why spend the money?"

"Come on. Would you build a new house without hiring an architect?"

"Why not?" One thing Shirley has never lacked is confidence.

I have strong persuasive powers, however. In this case, "no designer, no money" worked quite effectively. Shirley conceded the point.

We found Beth through some friends. She had three main attractions:

She'd done a great job for them.

She was just starting out so she had time available.

She hadn't yet passed all her courses so she wasn't pricey.

(An environmental design program takes four years of full-time study to complete; after that it takes another three years and an arduous set of exams to earn a National Council for Interior Design qualification. That's about the same length of time as it takes to become a doctor. It's a good thing they aren't paid accordingly.)

Beth came to our house for an initial meeting. I'm still not sure who was interviewing whom but I have a feeling that if we hadn't passed inspection she would have told us to look elsewhere.

During the course of that meeting Beth explained how she charged for her services. Now I know a thing or two about money but, frankly, I'm still not sure how designers' fees work. Maybe that's because there are so many different ways they can get paid, depending on how they operate and how well you negotiate.

Beth explained how she worked.

For starters, there would be a basic hourly rate. If she goes shopping with Shirley, she gets paid for her time. (Imagine getting paid for going shopping! Many women I know would kill for a job like that! Some men too!)

She would also collect a commission when you buy something through her. That's where matters start getting confusing. Beth has explained it to me several times and, if I understand her correctly, it works something like this:

If she buys something for you at retail, she gets a designer's discount off the retail price, which creates a net selling price, which is then marked up by a smaller percentage than the original discount to give the designer a commission, which creates a net net selling price, which is still lower than you would have paid had you purchased the item yourself in the store.

On the other hand, if the original price was quoted at wholesale, the designer marks it up by the amount of her commission, creating a net selling price to you which is somewhere between the wholesale price and the retail price, if the item were available at retail, which it often is not.

Is that all clear? No? I can't imagine why not.

Well, look at it this way – whatever the designer's cut, you still pay less than if you'd made the purchase yourself at retail prices. Or at least that's the way it should work out. It's a good idea to do some comparison shopping occasionally to be sure. Most designers, like Beth, are very scrupulous about this sort of thing but there are a few who will take advantage of this strange pricing structure.

Take the case of the couple who were looking for an oriental carpet. Their designer found a beauty – a perfect colour match for their decor. She sent them out to the supplier to have a look – but before she did she told the astonished carpet dealer to double the price. The couple liked what they saw. It seemed very expensive but the designer assured them it was good value. They made the purchase. She received twice the commission she would have earned on the original price of the rug, plus a split of the extra profit with the rug merchant! The various provincial interior designers' associations have established codes of ethics to avoid such rip-offs but every cluster has a few rotten grapes.

(The way to avoid such problems is to educate yourself. If you're buying an oriental rug, for example, look at the back side. In the best carpets, you'll find the pattern is just as bright as on the front. Also count the knots per square inch; the more the better. When you start getting into the hundreds, your eyesight will begin to blur and you'll know you have a good carpet.)

Anyway, after a long discussion, Beth decided she could live with us. We signed a letter of agreement and she went to work.

"You guys make all the decisions," I said casually. "I don't know about any of this stuff. Just tell me what it's going to cost."

A designer's dream, that's me.

A week later Beth came back with a colour scheme for our en suite bathroom renovation. I was called in for a look, just as a courtesy.

I had a few mild observations.

"Dusty rose! With peach highlights! In my bathroom? Over my dead body!"

The bathroom ended up grey marble and white. Much better. Oh yeah, there are still a few peach highlights. But they're hardly noticeable, as long as I shut my eyes.

I later learned this is typical. Husbands are always willing to let wives and designers do their thing – until they get a look at what they plan to do. Then they suddenly come out of the closet.

In fact, the relationship between husband and designer is often an adversarial one. The good designer understands this and adjusts accordingly.

For instance, I made it clear to Beth exactly how I wanted my office to look. Distinguished. Olde English. Dark wood everywhere – oak, perhaps mahogany. A massive desk with a black leather executive chair and burgundy leather side chairs with brass buttons. Wooden filing cabinets. Floor to ceiling dark wood bookcases. A credenza. Perhaps a world globe for atmosphere. Elegant.

Ponderous, Beth said.

My office is now complete. Grey steel desk with a flecked darker grey top. Matching grey steel filing cabinets. Blue-grey carpeting. The side chairs are grey with a burgundy stripe. I did get some floor to ceiling oak bookcases, however they're washed with a flint blue colour. (The manufacturers had never tried anything like that before. It turned out so well they now promote it in their catalogue as "Pape Blue". How many people have had a colour named after them?)

Believe it or not, the whole combination flows together harmoniously. Everyone who sees it comments on my good taste.

Well, hey, what are designers for?

I don't know if they teach it in design school, but if there isn't a course on how to deal with know-it-all-husbands, there should be.

Beth has certainly mastered the art.

The designer's first priority is to understand exactly what the husband means when he says he'll leave it all up to you.

There are three possibilities:

1) He really does mean it. This assumption should be made only if he's planning a three-year expedition to Antarctica.

2) He thinks he means it. This is a workable situation but one that involves a great deal of tact on the designer's part.

3) He intends to make every decision himself. In this case, the designer can learn to be a good yes-person or resign. The good ones will choose the latter.

I fell into category two – opinionated but manageable with patience.

Beth soon learned what pushed my off buttons. Floral patterns, rose carpeting and melon tiles quickly disappeared from her repertoire. Cool greys, soft blues and mellow greens took their place.

As Shirley had learned years before (I suspect there may have been some collaboration here), she also discovered that the water drip approach was more effective than the frontal assault in changing my firmly entrenched positions. It took two years for me to come to the conclusion that a mahogany suite might really not be the most practical, or the most attractive, alternative for my office. I'm still not sure exactly how she managed that.

Like most good designers, Beth sticks to her position

when she believes she's right. She has to; if she gives in and the ultimate result is a nightmarish hodge-podge, she's the one who gets the blame. Sure, that's unfair. Who ever said customers had to be fair?

But she also knows when to beat a strategic retreat, as she did with our bathroom. There's a difference between retreat and surrender, of course. She didn't let me dictate how the bathroom would look (thank heaven). She simply came back with a colour scheme I could live with.

One great advantage of working with an interior designer is that they see things differently from you. For instance, we never quite understood why we got so irritated when the kids ran in and out in the evening while we were watching TV. It was only when Beth pointed out that the traffic flow to the back door was directly between our chairs and the television set that we twigged.

Often, just a simple change in furniture positioning can make a room more comfortable. We'd always found it difficult to carry on conversations with guests across the length of our twenty-four foot living room. We also felt the dining room was too small. Beth solved both problems by moving the hutch cupboard from the dining room to the far living room wall and tightening up the sofa and chair grouping. We'd just lived with the old pattern too long to see how to change it.

But no matter how capable the designer, you always have to expect the unexpected.

Beth told us she once ordered a new Dhurri rug for a client. It was shipped directly from India – apparently packed in cow dung. For good luck? To preserve it? As a joke?

Whatever the reason, it was somewhat akin to having a skunk in the house.

"Every few days I'd call to see how it was," she told me. "It took weeks for the smell to abate. I'm amazed they were able to stay in the house. I'm even more amazed they still speak to me."

On another occasion, she ordered thirty-five yards of expensive material to upholster some living room furniture. The fabric was dutifully delivered to an upholsterer selected by the client who then left to go on vacation. When the client returned and called to have the furniture picked up, she received a "this number is no longer in service" message. The upholsterer had gone belly-up and disappeared. The pricey fabric was never seen again. About the only bright side to the story was that he didn't have the furniture too!

We had our share of these surprises. One example: the bathroom faucets arrived minus one drain assembly. The retailer insisted it had been in the box. Beth also insisted it was there when she'd checked it before shipping. The plumber insisted it had never arrived. Why anyone would want to swipe a drain assembly is beyond me but somehow it had vanished. Words flew. Finally, Shirley stepped in and negotiated a settlement to the dispute using a simple technique: she bought a new one. At forty dollars, she figured it was cheaper than paying for the time it was taking for the plumber to argue about who was at fault.

Sometimes it's the little expenses that get to you during renovations. People will pay contractors hundreds of extra dollars without a whimper simply by being told: "We found something we weren't expecting behind that wall." They never tell you exactly what it is they found. A skeleton? A treasure chest? Someone's old lunch bag? All we learn is that, whatever it is, it wasn't anticipated so it will cost more.

Designers moan over the ease with which contractors can extract more money from clients who then turn around and try to make it up by cutting decorating costs.

Delivery costs are a favourite target. It doesn't matter that the furniture was bought at a big discount; clients expect it to arrive at the front door free. When they find a modest delivery charge added to the bill, they scream.

I heard of one couple who were so angry about being charged for delivery from a factory thirty miles away that they decided to pick up the chair themselves. The husband wrestled it out to his car, secured it in the open trunk with some light rope, and set out to drive home. By the time he hit sixty, the wind pressure was too much. The chair broke loose and ended up in splinters in the middle of a six-lane expressway. Again, there was one bright side. The cars following managed to avoid colliding with it, thus averting what could have been a huge liability suit.

So is hiring a designer a good idea? Looking back on it now, I believe Shirley was right when she told me she could have done it herself – with my help, of course. I'm also convinced that if we had done it that way, we'd either have moved or been divorced by now – perhaps both.

Thanks, Beth.

It Costs What?

It never occurred to me that faucets cost money.

That's probably because I'd never bought any before.

They were always just *there*. They came with the house. I never thought anything about them. When you move into a new home, you expect to find faucets attached to the sinks and wash basins. I never even noticed what they looked like so long as when I gave them a turn, water appeared.

Using this criterion, I guess I unconsciously assumed that all sorts of things are free. Sinks. Drains. Medicine cabinets. Bathtubs. Lighting fixtures. Towel bars. Soap dishes. Unless you're building a new home, you take it for granted these will all be present when you arrive.

I mean, can you imagine walking into a home you've just purchased to find the previous owners took the toilets when they left?

That's why I was so surprised when Shirley and Beth came to me and said it was time to go faucet shopping.

Faucet shopping? She might as well have been asking me to go look at furnace filters with her. People don't *shop* for that kind of stuff.

After all, what's there to look at? All faucets are the same; they're made of chrome and turn on and off.

Beth stared at me in horror. Clearly, she still hadn't grasped the full depth of my philistinism in matters of home decor.

I put off Shirley as long as possible; then, one morning, she forced the issue at breakfast when she noticed my attention had strayed momentarily from reading the cereal box.

"The plumber's coming next week."

"Uh-huh."

"He's going to be installing a new sink in the bathroom."

"Uh-huh."

"He's going to be taking away all our old stuff."

"Uh-huh."

"I just wondered how high you wanted the fountains."

"Fountains? You and Beth are putting fountains in our bathroom?"

"Well, we hadn't actually planned it that way. But since we don't have any taps, that's what we'll end up with."

"Fountains?"

"That's one of the things faucets do, dear. They hold the water in the pipes. But I'm sure you'll get used to the splashing sound. You may even find it lulls you to sleep. Of course, it'll make washing your hands a different experience."

"Why don't we just use our old taps?"

"They don't fit."

"Why didn't we buy a sink they *did* fit?"

"Because they stopped making them twenty years ago."

"Oh."

I went with her to the faucet store. Actually, they also sold a lot of other exciting things, like shower heads and toilet paper holders. But that day Shirley only had eyes for faucets.

I couldn't believe the array. There were gold faucets, chrome faucets, porcelain faucets, silver faucets, copper faucets, brass faucets, marble faucets, oak faucets. There were faucets that mixed your hot and cold water and faucets that gave it to you straight. There were Colonial faucets, French Provincial faucets, Art Deco faucets, neo-Gothic faucets, Georgian faucets, contemporary faucets. I didn't notice any Palaeolithic faucets but I'm sure some would have materialized if I'd asked.

There were square taps, lever taps, cross-handled taps, oval taps and hexagonal taps.

There were white sets, black sets, red sets, turquoise sets, antique brass sets and flowered sets.

I looked at faucets shaped like wings, faucets shaped like angels, swan's neck faucets and porpoise faucets. I saw faucets with interchangeable handles – if you get tired of one style, you just switch it.

"I like these," I said, pointing to a set of faucets in the image of two curvaceous unclothed ladies.

Shirley looked at me in disgust and muttered something like: "Get serious."

"Hey, I can think of worse things to look at first thing in the morning," I muttered, after I was sure her attention had been diverted elsewhere.

I came across an old-fashioned set of faucets with "H" and "C" on them – the only such ones in evidence.

"How much are these things?" I asked. There were no price tags attached.

"We'll have to get a price list from the saleslady," Shirley said. "She's over there."

I got the list. Shirley should have warned me to sit down before I looked at it. There wasn't a number under three hundred. Many of them were into the thousands.

"No, no, we don't want a complete bathroom set," I protested to the saleslady. "Just some faucets."

She smiled as if she thought I was trying to make a joke. I realized with a chill that the prices I was looking at were indeed for faucets only.

"Uh, have you thought about going to Canadian Tire?" I asked Shirley.

"Don't be silly. They only have inexpensive stuff there."

That would be nice, I thought. But I kept silent.

At least for a while. Then I came across a set I actually liked.

"These are nice."

"Yes, but they're European."

"So?"

"Plumbers don't like to install European faucets."

"For heaven's sake, why not?"

"They're too complicated."

"How?"

"They have straight screws. For some reason, our plumbers can only seem to deal with tapered screws. They see a straight screw and they fall to pieces."

"That's the craziest thing I ever heard."

"I agree, but that's how it is."

"So what faucets should I be looking for?"

"Moen."

"Like the one in the kitchen we threw out?"

"That's it."

"Moen. It sounds German or Swedish."

"It's not. Maybe they just gave it that name to make the line seem more fashionable. Actually, it's made in the U.S.A. By a company called Masco."

"So let me get this straight. Our plumbers hate European faucets but people think they're trendy so a North American company gives their faucet a European-sounding name so they'll sell better and the plumbers don't mind because they're not really European at all. Have I got that right?"

"Exactly."

"Geez."

Shirley couldn't find exactly what she wanted so we went to another store. Here they had a large collection of faucets displayed in individual glass cases. It was like being in a faucet museum.

There was a pink onyx and brass set with a price tag of more than nine hundred dollars. A set with handcut crystal taps and a gold-plated spout was almost fifteen hundred dollars. For a thousand more, we could get a modern crystal and bronze design that looked like a truncated skateboard.

I tried to divert her attention elsewhere. Like out the door.

Finally, she found something she liked.

"Aren't these pretty? They'll go perfectly with the decor." She was pointing at two classically styled gold-coloured taps with a separate spout and a pop-up drain assembly.

"And they're on sale . . ."

"I love them."

". . . for only six hundred dollars."

"I don't think they're quite right. What about these?"

By now I'd recovered my composure and carefully reviewed the price list. I pointed her in the direction of some utilitarian chrome faucets that looked just fine to me, at half the price.

She gave me the same look I'd received from the saleslady earlier. One of the secrets of a long-lasting marriage is to know when you're licked.

"Fine," I said. "I think the gold ones are great. But you didn't really need to drag me out here to choose them."

"Sure I did," she replied. "Just think what your reaction would have been if I'd walked in and announced I'd just bought a six hundred dollar faucet set. You'd have hit the roof.

Now you know what the real world is like."

"Fine. Can we go?"

"Oh, no. Now we have to look for a matching tooth-brush holder and robe hook and. . ."

By the time she'd finished, we'd spent several hundred dollars more. The irony is we still keep the toothbrushes in a plastic glass. Shirley doesn't want the two hundred dollar holder mucked up.

Later, I asked a friend in the building supplies business why simple bathroom items cost so much.

"They don't, if you go to Home Depot or Aikenhead's," he said. "But you have to realize that when you go to those bath boutiques, you're not really buying faucets. You're paying for works of art."

I think about that whenever I wash my hands. Some-how, I'm not convinced.

Guess What, Mike,
The Ceiling's Leaking Again

If I ever go house-hunting again, the first thing I'm going to do is turn on all the showers and let them run for an hour; then I'm going to inspect the ceilings of the rooms directly beneath them with a magnifying glass. If there's the slightest hint of moisture, it's off the list. I've had my fill of bathrooms that manage to send their water everywhere but down the drain.

We've owned three homes and all of them have had leaky shower stalls. It's reached the point where I'm beginning to suspect a plumbers' union conspiracy. Build every house with at least one leaky shower. Think of the business it will generate.

The house on Woodsworth Road was the worst by far. It gave us not one but two leaking bathrooms for our money.

Admittedly, the leak in the main bathroom wasn't too bad. It was so slow it took a couple of years to ruin the ceiling below.

But the one in our bedroom en suite was a veritable gusher. Run the shower for five minutes and the room below resembled a tropical thunderstorm. We hadn't seen any evidence of this when we inspected the house. Either the ceiling had been recently replastered or the previous owners never used the shower.

But it didn't take us long to discover we had a big problem on our hands. One day in fact.

The room below the shower had been designated as Kim's bedroom. The day after we moved in, a Saturday morning, I arose and went to take my first shower in our lovely new home. I was happily soaping myself in the hot water when the bathroom door burst open.

"Turn it off," Shirley yelled.

"What? Why?"

"Just turn it off! Now!"

She had that "don't mess with me" tone in her voice. I turned off the water, wrapped myself in a towel, and went out into the bedroom. There was Kim, soaking wet and wailing. She'd been taking a shower at the same time as me. The problem was she had still been in bed.

Naturally, we called in a plumber. He examined the situation.

"Grouting," he declared.

"Grouting?"

"Yep. That's your problem. See here." He ran his finger between the tiles. "Grouting disintegrating. Got a couple of bad tiles there too. And you're probably getting some leakage around that soap dish. I can fix it okay, be as good as new."

He did the work. I started taking showers again.

A few mornings later Kim joined me. Again, while she was still in bed.

We called another plumber.

"It's the pan. Probably got a hole in it. I'll have to install a new one."

"But doesn't that mean ripping out all the tiles?"

"Yeah. I'll have to replace those too."

"But we just paid to have all the tiles grouted."

He shrugged. Plumbers couldn't care less about that sort of thing.

It took three working days. He ripped out the tiles, removed the old pan, put in a new one, and retiled everything.

Huge mess. Huge money.

But it seemed to work. We ran the water for an hour or so, and nothing happened to Kim's ceiling. The plumber proclaimed success.

By now it was our first winter in the house and I had discovered another shower problem. It seems the original builder ran out of insulation about the time the exterior wall in the vicinity of what was to be our en suite shower was being finished. Rather than wait for a new shipment, the workmen went ahead and closed it in.

As a result, getting into the stall on a cold day was roughly equivalent to taking a shower in a refrigerator. I switched my morning ablutions to the main bathroom for the duration.

This meant the shower repairs didn't receive a true test until spring. After three mornings of using the stall again, the drips were back.

I moaned about the problem to our next door neighbour.

"I have exactly the same thing," he told me. "I've tried four different plumbers. None of them could fix it. In fact, I ended up in small claims court with the last one."

I relayed this encouraging news to Shirley.

"Maybe we'd just better forget it," she said. "You've gotten used to the other bathroom anyway. So the kids are lined up outside the door."

We did as she suggested. For the next few years, the shower stall remained unused except at Christmas time; then it became a handy hiding place for the kids' gifts. In that role it was highly successful; they told us years later it was the one place it never occurred to them to look because they thought we were still using the shower on a regular basis.

The rest of the year the stall gathered cobwebs – literally. We wouldn't even look behind the shower curtain from one month to the next; when we did take a peek we found it resembled what Miss Havisham's bathroom would have looked like if Dickens had bothered to describe it.

Then came the big renovation. The en suite was to be completely rebuilt by the same contractor who was doing the kitchen. The supervisor was a pleasant young man named Mike.

We told him from the outset that repairing the shower stall leak was an absolutely essential part of the job.

"No problem," he said.

We described the previous attempts to stop the water flow.

"No problem," he said.

We told him about our next door neighbour.

"No problem," he said.

Beth drew up a written list of priorities for the work, including fixing the leak.

"No problem," he said.

By this point he was getting a little exasperated about our obsession with the matter.

"I guarantee it will be done to your complete satisfaction. Okay?"

Those words were to come back to haunt him.

The plumber came, an irascible man named Sam, who seemed more interested in playing golf than plumbing.

"Heading down to Myrtle Beach next week," he told

Shirley. "Got a time share there. But don't worry. It'll all get done before I go."

It did. He tore out the old stall entirely. He ripped out all the old piping, installed a new pan, put in brand new fixtures (North American made of course), and left to go south.

The tile man arrived and installed our expensive marble tile.

The shower stall looked like a million bucks. I felt that's about what it had cost.

The first day after it was completed, I took a long shower.

No problem!

The second day after it was completed, I took a long shower.

No problem!

The third day after it was completed, I took a long shower.

"You'd better come downstairs," Shirley said when I got out.

I did. Drops of water were gently falling into the pans she had spread around.

Shirley called Mike.

"It can't be."

"It is."

"I'll send Sam."

Sam was still off playing golf but his son came. He cut a hole in Kim's ceiling and probed around inside.

"It's wet all right," he pronounced.

"No kidding."

He inspected the new piping carefully.

"Aha!"

"What?"

"There's a pinhole in the main pipe."

"The *new* main pipe? How can that be?"

"It happens. I'll solder it and it'll be fine."

He did. Mike sent in his plasterer to repair the hole in the ceiling and repaint.

I took three showers. Shirley went down each morning to inspect.

On the third day, she was waiting when I came out of the bathroom.

"Guess what," she said.

She called Mike.

"The ceiling's leaking again."

"No."

"Yes."

By now Sam was back from Myrtle Beach. He cut another hole in Kim's ceiling. He inspected all the plumbing and proclaimed it to be sound.

"Must be the tile man's fault," he said. "Did a bad job of installation and it's leaking."

Shirley called Mike.

"Sam says it's the tile man's fault."

"It can't be."

"That's what Sam says."

Huge sigh. "Okay, I'll send him out."

At this point I was feeling very thankful that Beth had insisted on mentioning the leak in writing.

The tile man arrived. Surprisingly, he did find a defective tile and some grouting that wasn't up to snuff. He fixed it all and pronounced the shower to be "A-okay."

The plasterer came back to repair the ceiling hole.

I took a shower. Nothing.

I took a second shower. Nothing.

I took a third shower. Still nothing.

We opened a bottle of Champagne in celebration. Kim put away her bedside towel.

Three months later, Shirley happened to glance at the ceiling. There was a big dark spot there.

"Mike, the shower's leaking again."

"It can't be. Oh, Mrs. Pape, it can't be. Please tell me you're kidding. Sam's not speaking to me anymore."

"It is."

Sam came yet again.

"I was supposed to be playing golf this afternoon," he muttered.

"Tough," Shirley said. Customers can be so uncaring sometimes.

He cut another hole in the ceiling. He inspected everything.

"I can't believe this," he announced after an hour. "Everything's fine. The pipes are fine. The fixtures are fine. The tiles are fine. It can't be leaking."

"It is."

"Have you considered ghosts?"

"Ha ha." We were long past the point of being amused.

"Well, there is one thing I could try," he conceded.

"Please do."

He unscrewed the faucets.

"I know they're new," he explained. "But they've been taken off so many times to be checked the threads may have worn. Some water could be leaking out that way."

He took out two rubber bands, wrapped one around each of the threads to create a seal, and reattached the faucets.

"If this doesn't work. . ." He left the rest of the sentence unfinished. I'm not sure what was in his mind but it may have involved dynamite.

The plasterer came back. We'd seen him so often he was now like part of the family.

The ceiling was fixed. I took a shower.

I'm still taking them. We haven't seen Sam since that day.

I hope he's enjoying his golf games. He earned them.

Pack the Fish Dear, We're Moving

They don't make furniture like they used to. Perhaps that's why we're so attached to what we have. So attached, in fact, that we can't bear to part with any of it.

We started building a furniture collection even before we were married. As I was approaching the end of a year's post-graduate study in Toulouse, France, I wrote Shirley (overseas phone calls in those days were far beyond the affordability of a poor student) with an offer I thought she couldn't refuse.

Fly over in May, we'll get married here, and spend the summer camping around Europe, I romantically proposed. All you'll have to pay is your own air fare (I said I was poor, didn't I?).

Now, Shirley has always been a highly practical person. So she assessed the situation carefully and then did what any practical person presented with this proposition would do: she spent her air fare money on a new Krohler sofa.

I think she was afraid that if we started life together in a tent we'd be living under canvas for years. Furniture offered more stability than I did at that point.

At the time, I thought she was nuts. She was turning her back on the opportunity of a lifetime. (No, not marrying me. Camping around Europe.)

Now I'm not so sure. We had that sofa for more than thirty years. During that time she's been to Europe with me on many occasions – and never once slept in a tent!

We were married in Montreal the following spring. Shortly before the wedding we made our first joint furniture purchase – our bed.

I had decided I wanted one of the new king-size beds that were becoming popular. The salesman at Eaton's was dubious.

"Most apartments don't have large enough bedrooms," he pointed out. "And you may have trouble getting it through the door. Why don't you just push twins together? Gives you a lot more flexibility."

Here we were, just about to be married, and he wanted to put us into twin beds! I wondered if he had any children.

We bought the king-size. After that, every place we moved into was judged not on the price or the location, but on whether or not the master bedroom was large enough for our oversized playground.

During the early years of our marriage, Shirley continued to spend money on furniture. Since I was making very
little as a reporter with *The Gazette* of Montreal (my starting
salary in 1962 was sixty dollars a week), I tried to convince her
to buy cheap stuff.

She never argued the point. She just ignored me.

In those days, some of the finest rock maple furniture in
the world was made by a company called Vilas based in the
Eastern Townships of Quebec. Their products were well-
designed, superbly crafted, and built to last forever. This was
what Shirley decided she wanted despite my howls of protest.

"Three hundred dollars for a dining room table? That's
robbery! I won't pay it!"

That was in the mid-sixties. We're still eating off that
same table today. Shirley knew what she was doing.

She bought Vilas coffee tables, end tables, bookcases,
desks and chairs. She added a hutch cupboard and server to
her collection. There were Vilas chests and bureaus. The only
thing that stopped her was that the company went out of
business. I was amazed. I thought that Shirley was single-
handedly keeping their factory operating three shifts.

We didn't eat and never went out but we filled our tiny
apartment rooms with fine furniture.

My job had me being transferred to a new city about
once every three years. My managing editor wasn't amused by
the moving bills.

Then things got worse. We went fishing.

We'd never really taken a honeymoon – Shirley had dedicated
all our income to keeping the Vilas company solvent.

But Quebec City, where I was posted at the time, does
a clever imitation of Siberia in winter. We decided to use the
Christmas bonus for a week's holiday in Miami Beach.

Miami was a different place in the sixties. You could
actually walk the streets at night. The restaurants were cheap
(they had to compete with hotel package deals for business)
and the beach was clean.

We basked in the sun for six days and decided to cap the

vacation with a final treat – an ocean fishing trip.

I had recently read Hemingway's *The Old Man and The Sea* and pictured myself battling a thousand-pound blue marlin out in the Gulf Stream. Unfortunately, when we checked out the prices of deep sea charter boats, we realized they were far out of our range. A hundred dollars a day? Wow!

All we could afford was a party fishing boat that ventured no farther than Miami harbour. The cost was five dollars for the two of us.

"That's more like it," Shirley said. Little did she know what awaited.

It was one of those drift fishing boats that went out just far enough to catch a current. At that point, the captain turned off the engine (saving fuel costs in the process, of course) and ordered everyone to the starboard side where we cast shrimp-baited lines into the water.

The kids had fun pulling in small snapper. I was bored. This was hardly the blue marlin league.

Then everything exploded!

Atlantic sailfish tend to travel in small groups. Three of them were cruising along just below the surface, leisurely feeding, when they ran into what appeared to be a school of shrimp – except all these shrimps had hooks attached to them. The rod in my hand suddenly gave a tremendous jolt and the next thing I knew a huge fish was breaking water about a hundred feet from the boat. And then another! And then another!

We had hooked three sailfish simultaneously!

The captain screamed at everyone else to bring their lines in. My fish broke water again, shaking furiously to throw off the hook; then it crashed back into the waves and the line starting screaming off the reel.

"Get the rod tip up! Hold him! Try to turn him! No, not that way! Haven't you ever caught a fish before?"

"Not one like this," I muttered. The muscle in my right arm felt as if it were twice its normal size.

"Watch out, he's coming back up. Don't give him any slack! Reel! Reel!"

The sailfish broke water again. A vision of Hemingway's Old Man flashed through my head. Damn it, I was going to have this fish!

The boat wasn't equipped with a fishing chair. After all, we weren't supposed to catch anything larger than a sheepshead. Why go to the expense of installing a chair?

So I had to fight the fish standing at the rail, the butt of the rod jammed into my stomach. (I bore the bruise with pride for weeks after.)

It lasted more than half an hour. At the end, I was more exhausted than I had ever been in my life. But the fish was alongside, the mate was leaning over with the gaff, and we had it! It was in the boat!

"You'll want it mounted, of course," the captain said, eyes gleaming at the commission he was about to make.

"Of course!"

"It'll only cost two hundred dollars."

"Of course," I said weakly.

That's how George joined our family.

That's what we named him when we hung him in the living room of our apartment. Shirley wasn't thrilled with the idea of a seven-foot sailfish dominating our decor but I was adamant.

"He's beautiful," I enthused. "Plus, he cost two hundred dollars."

After that George went where we went. When we were transferred to Ottawa, the moving company had to build a special crate for him at a cost that made my long-suffering managing editor turn blue.

"We paid that much to move a damn fish?"

"Hey, sending me to Ottawa was your idea, not mine."

"You. Your wife. Your furniture. Your gerbils. Not a seven-foot fish."

"Just consider him part of our family."

Three years later, the Southam organization asked me to become their bureau chief in England.

"They suggest we put our furniture in storage and take

a furnished flat in London," I told Shirley.

"How long will we be there?"

"A minimum of three years. Maybe as long as five."

"We're taking our things with us. But we can store George."

"If the rest goes, George goes too."

Years later, we tell the story of our move to London and laugh. At the time, it was a domestic nightmare. I'm amazed the marriage survived.

It began as soon as we stepped off the plane. We'd been booked into a two-bedroom furnished flat in the Shepherd's Market section of Mayfair, where we were supposed to stay for a month while we located a permanent place and our furniture arrived from Canada.

You don't tend to sleep much on an overnight flight in economy class, especially when you're accompanied by a three-year-old child who suffers from motion sickness and a newborn baby. So by the time we disembarked at Heathrow, we were exhausted. Kim, who to our surprise had managed to contain herself on the plane, then proceeded to throw up at the feet of the immigration official, earning us a speedy passage through the airport bureaucracy.

When we finally arrived at the flat, we were running on empty. The smell of rancid olive oil in the hall as we made our way down the corridor didn't help.

"It'll be fine when we get inside," I assured my wife.

"It better be."

It wasn't.

The sink was full of dirty dishes. The toilet appeared not to have been flushed in a week. The linen on the beds was filthy. The fridge was filled with rotting food. The rooms appeared to have last been cleaned sometime prior to the Second World War. There was a month's worth of garbage in one corner. And there were other living creatures inhabiting the flat besides us.

Shirley sat down on a creaky chair and stared at me. I saw one big tear roll down her face.

"I want to go home."

The children wailed.

"But we don't have a home any more," I rationalized.

"I don't care. I'm not staying here."

The children wailed some more.

We managed to get someone to come in and clean the place; then we discovered that our location was smack in the middle of one of London's red light districts. A fashionable red light district, mind you. The ladies didn't walk the streets; they just displayed their names in large letters above well-lit doorbells. Lulu. Fifi. Belle. A few even had signs to subtly communicate their specialities. "French lessons." "Greek spoken." "Mistress of Discipline." I wasn't even sure what they all meant. I was just glad the kids couldn't read yet.

"I'm not staying here," Shirley said firmly.

"But our furniture won't arrive for another three weeks."

"I don't care. We're getting out. Now."

We started to look.

Flat-hunting in London is a unique experience. Never have I seen so many uninhabitable accommodations commanding such outrageous prices.

We saw flats so damp there were mushrooms growing from the walls. We looked at basement flats that had never seen sunlight. We saw flats that made our temporary accommodation seem sparkling clean. At one place, the owners served us the best gin-and-tonic I've ever tasted. But Shirley looked at the open, unscreened windows and the street three floors below and decided this was not where she wanted to raise young children.

"I want to go home," she said, after two dozen strikeouts.

"This *is* home," I reminded her.

Finally, we found something. We stumbled on it by accident; the friend of a friend of a friend heard of a place that *might* be coming open (that was about the only way to find anything half-decent in London in those days). It was located in a district called Swiss Cottage, sandwiched between St. John's Wood, where the Beatles cut their records, and toney Hampstead. We went round for a look.

The flat was in a once-fashionable building that still retained an air of pretention, mainly consisting of doormen who would deign to bid you good morning in exchange for a healthy tip.

It was on two levels, reflecting its pre-war construction. The upper level was for the family. The lower level, which incorporated the kitchen, was for the live-in help.

We didn't initially see it that way, of course. All we saw was a lot of space for our growing family in what seemed to be a clean building in a good neighbourhood.

There was just one catch. To get the place, we had to make an under-the-table payment to the sitting tenant of several thousand pounds. Technically, demands for key money in rent-controlled London were illegal. But such was the demand for desirable accommodation that it went on all the time. If we wanted the place, we had no option. We paid.

We did get some fixtures, fittings and furniture as part of the deal, including rugs, drapes and an old grandfather clock that never worked and still doesn't. As it turned out, that was all the furniture we had on the day we moved in.

The saga of George and the rest of our possessions began the week after we flew to England. Unbeknownst to us, Montreal's longshoremen went out on strike before our chattels had been loaded onto the freighter that was to bring them over.

The strike went on for weeks. While we were labouring under the delusion that our possessions were somewhere in the middle of the North Atlantic, they were in fact sitting on the dockside in Montreal while negotiations dragged on.

We only learned about this when we called the moving company.

"We've found a flat and will be moving in next Friday," I brightly announced. "Would you please arrange to have our furniture delivered first thing that morning."

"What did you say your name was again?"

I told her.

"Sorry, luv, I can't seem to find the file. Hang on a sec."

A few moments later, a dignified male voice came on the line.

"Ah yes, Mr. Pape. Seems we've had a bit of a problem here. Can't understand why no one's been in touch with you before now. It's about this strike in Montreal. . ."

Panic time. Shirley picked up the phone and called Harrod's, on the theory that if any store in London could solve our problem, they could.

"No, madam, we do not rent furniture," she was told. "But I can give you the name of a company that does."

Have you ever wondered where stage productions get all their props? Okay, I confess I hadn't either. But we found out the next day.

The company Harrod's had referred us to was a theatrical supplies organization with a warehouse that was as big as an airport terminal in the suburb of Horsham. We wandered through it discussing whether we should furnish the flat in French Provincial, English Georgian or Spanish Moorish. There were furniture settings for Scottish castles, Swiss chalets and Tahitian grass huts. If we had desired, we could have made our flat look like a scene from the decadent South (*Cat on a Hot Tin Roof*) or an English seaside resort (*Separate Tables*).

"And how long do you expect the run to be?" asked the kindly, white-bearded gentleman who was proudly showing us around.

We explained the situation. He was flustered.

"A private flat? Oh my, I don't know. We've never done anything like that."

I assured him we'd take good care of the furniture. He looked dubious.

We found a room setting we liked.

"How much?" I asked.

He told me. The colour drained from my face.

"I assure you, that's quite reasonable," he said. "Just think of it, Laurence Olivier sat in this very chair."

"How much for one that a bit player used?"

He didn't get my point.

We compromised on the bare necessities – beds, a crib, a kitchen table, a sofa and a few chairs.

"But you have nothing for your dining room," he protested. "Look at this fine oak table over here. Note the intricate carving."

I said we weren't planning on doing any entertaining for a while. The look on his face showed his reaction to that: "Colonials!"

The rented furniture arrived and we settled in, sort of. Life wasn't exactly normal, however. One day my shoelace broke and I asked Shirley where I could find another.

"In the top drawer of your dresser."

"But we don't have my dresser."

"Then you'll have to wait until it comes. I'm not buying things we already have."

This policy led to the kids becoming housebound as summer moved into autumn ("their warm clothes will come soon"). We turned down invitations to formal dinner parties ("why rent a tux when you own one?"). We scrubbed plans for a weekend in the country ("our clothes are in the container"). I was just relieved that Shirley decided it was okay to buy toilet paper.

Finally, the good news came.

"Ah yes, Mr. Pape, I'm pleased to inform you your container has arrived. We'll bring it around Thursday morning if that's convenient."

It was. We called the theatrical supply company. They arrived bright and early Thursday to remove their furniture. It was only when their truck was about to pull out of the courtyard that it occurred to me our stuff should have shown up by now.

"Hang on a sec," I told the driver. "Let me just check."

"What did you say your name was?" It was a different voice on the other end of the line. I told him.

"Pape. Pape. No, nothing going out today. May be tied up in customs. Check back in a week or so."

I yelled at him. All I got was: "Sorry, guv."

Shirley yelled to the driver from the theatrical company. "Bring it all back!"

"Back, mum?" His suspicion that all North Americans are mad was being confirmed.

"Back. In here. Now."

"Can't."

"Why?"

"Got to take it back to Horsham. Says so right here." He displayed his waybill.

"But we don't want it to go back now."

"Says here you do."

"We've changed our minds."

"Sorry." He gunned the truck and left. In Britain, when something is written, it's carved in stone. There's no point arguing about it.

We called the theatrical supply firm. A few hours later the driver was back with new written instructions. The furniture went back in the flat.

Two weeks later, our container finally arrived. Somewhere along the way, it had sprung a leak. Everything had been bathed in sea water. Our bed was soggy and green with mildew. The dining room table was cracked and warped. Chair cushions squished when we sat on them. Shirley's fur coat smelled like a wet dog.

Only George appeared unscathed. But then, he was a fish.

"I want to go home," my wife wailed. The children howled. The movers fled.

Faced with another crisis, Shirley did what she always did at such moments in London: she called Harrod's.

They came and took the bed to be recovered. They sent in a man who proved to be a wizard at repairing rock maple. They restored Shirley's coat and dehumidified the chair cushions.

After six months of misadventures, London was finally home.

Given all that history, perhaps you can understand my distress when, years later, Shirley announced that much of our furniture would have to go as part of the renovation process.

First, it was the sofa she'd traded her honeymoon in Europe for. I thought she'd cling to it for life but it was actually I who protested its departure.

"Fine, we'll keep it," she said when I whined. "Where do you suggest we put it?"

I had no answer. It went to Kendrew.

One of the advantages of seeing your children leave home and set up housekeeping on their own is that you can palm off old furniture on them. That way you're not really throwing it away. It's still in the family, after all. And the kids *do* need it.

Shirley effectively used this rationale to divest herself of almost everything she'd bought over the years and start afresh. Another sofa went to Kim and her husband. Kendrew got a hide-a-bed and some tables and chairs.

Even our king-size bed wasn't sacrosanct.

Actually, she'd been after me about that for around ten years.

"We need a new bed," she'd say every spring.

"Forget it," I growled. I had it in my mind that a bed should be for life.

Never mind that the foam mattress had deteriorated to the point where we had to put boards under it for support. So we woke up each morning with stiff necks and sore backs. It was our matrimonial bed. Changing it would be bad luck. It should last as long as the marriage.

I'd forgotten that most marriages don't last thirty years any more. Nor do beds.

It was only when I began to feel I was rolling down a hill in the middle of the night that I agreed to be dragged to a bedding store. Shirley reports that my mattress-testing reactions went something like this:

"Ahhhh."

"Umm-hmm."

"So soft."

"Comfy!"

When I ended up under the sheets and almost asleep on one of the beds in the store window, they pounced.

"Just sign here," the clerk said.

"We'll have it in a week," Shirley chimed in.

Still groggy, I was led from the store. I'm still not sure what happened. All I know is I now sleep better at night.

Changing all the furniture was not without mishap. Shirley and Beth decided on a new colour scheme for the living room, based on a fabric they had selected for the sofa. Everything was keyed off it – the carpeting, the other chair coverings, the drapes, even the new frames for the paintings.

Then Beth went in to place the order.

"Oh, didn't anyone tell you? That pattern's been discontinued. We don't have any more in stock."

Beth tried to find alternatives. She couldn't locate anything I liked. The whole living room went on hold. I thought of all the money I was saving and continued to reject each new pattern she produced.

It was Shirley who broke the impasse.

"Did I tell you? The living room furniture's going out next week."

"Out where?"

"To the kids. We promised it to them."

"But we still haven't chosen the new stuff."

"Then I guess we'll have an empty living room for a while."

I chose a fabric the next day.

But there was one issue on which I remained adamant. George. Despite Shirley's pleas, he wasn't going anywhere.

Granted, he was pretty battered from all the moving at this point. His huge dorsal fin was tattered, one of his tail fins was broken, and he looked bedraggled. But I remembered Hemingway and stuck up for him.

"We're not going to let the sharks get him."

"What are you talking about? We're just going to offer him to the kids."

"They won't want him." (I was right on that one.)

She resorted to the tactic that had worked so often before. "Fine. Where do you suggest we put him?"

This time I had an answer. "We'll build a special room for him."

We did. We also sent him out for a fin-lift. The taxidermist did a great restoration job. George now proudly hangs over the bar in our new games room, a constant reminder of that afternoon of drift fishing in Miami harbour so many years ago.

As the old Dean Martin song goes, memories are made of this.

The Wine Cellar from Hell

We all have our weaknesses. Mine is wine.

It has been ever since I was in high school. While the other guys thought it was macho to walk around with a flask of rye on their hip, I discovered early that a bottle of French white wine, fresh from cooling in a fast-rushing stream on a summer day, is just about the most powerful aphrodisiac known to man.

I've loved wine ever since.

Unfortunately, I was never in a position to pursue my interest seriously until we moved into the house. In fact, one of the things that clinched the sale was the cold room under the front stairs.

The original occupants had used it as a root cellar. It was a barren-looking spot with one naked light bulb and floor-to-ceiling industrial shelving to hold jars of preserves and sacks of potatoes. But I saw the possibilities immediately.

No sooner had we moved in than I was stocking those shelves with bottles of wine. Nothing elaborate – we couldn't afford the really expensive vintages. But I gradually built a respectable enough cellar that always managed to produce a bottle of Beaujolais for a summer barbecue or a gutsy chardonnay to accompany the Thanksgiving turkey.

The main problem with the cellar was the temperature. Wines are supposed to be stored at a constant fifty-five degrees Fahrenheit (about twelve Celsius for those who insist on using that confusing measurement) to keep them fresh and to ensure proper maturing. Our cellar temperature varied from the low forties on a cold winter morning to the mid-seventies in a summer heat wave. That's too much of a temperature swing as my friend, wine expert Tony Aspler, kept telling me.

So with all the rest of the house being torn apart, it was only natural our attention would turn at some point to the wine cellar.

Actually, it was Shirley who moved it up the priority scale. She wanted a place to stick an awkward, ugly piece of furniture, a cabinet/production table that had once served in the art department of a magazine where I worked. I'd purchased it to hold office supplies when the company went out of business.

It was a functional piece but it didn't fit in the great new scheme of things. She wanted to toss it out. Since I'm notoriously reluctant to get rid of anything (there's always a use sometime), we had to find somewhere to put it.

The wine cellar offered a solution. The cabinet would make a fine tasting table, while providing storage room for all my wine paraphernalia. But to make room for it we would have to tear out everything that was already in there – particularly those warehouse-green storage racks – and start over.

It would cost some money but, after the kitchen, it would be peanuts. Anyway, I was now adding some finer wines to my collection. They needed better storage conditions.

Besides, shelves just wouldn't do. They were awkward, what with all the bottles stacked on top of one another. I was losing track of what was at the bottom of the pile. Whenever I took the time to dig down, I inevitably discovered a vintage that should have been drunk years before and by now was useful only to flavour a salad.

So we agreed. It would be done.

We contacted a company that specialized in this sort of work. In due course a representative (I'll call him Fred to protect the guilty) arrived to assess our situation and give us a quote.

He walked around the cellar, tut-tutted a few times, and gave his verdict. The room would have to be climate-controlled. But before that could happen it needed to be properly insulated. That meant erecting a new exterior wall and putting in a proper floor. All the existing bins would come out, to be replaced by proper wine racks. A refrigeration system would be installed, although it would have to be in the furnace room immediately adjacent because of space requirements. And, of course, the offending table which had started all this would be moved in to serve for tastings and note-taking.

He did some calculations and presented me with his estimate. I gulped hard.

"How long will it take?"

"Couple of weeks. No more."

I looked at the cost again and told him to go ahead.

In early May, 1990 (the time frame is very important as

you'll see), the carpenter arrived. I forget his name (you'll soon understand why), but my wife immediately tagged him as "Jerome". I should have known we were in trouble when I saw his truck in the driveway. On it in huge letters was the name of his company: "We Fix You."

Clearly, Jerome's grasp of the English language wasn't so hot. But, heck, that didn't mean he was a bad carpenter.

Jerome dutifully set to work. I had already moved the wine bottles out of the cellar, storing them in a spare room. He shifted the now-empty bins to the garage, put in a new floor within a couple of days, and had the required wall erected in a week. So far so good.

That's when it all started to come unwound. Although I didn't realize it at the time, the Wine Cellar from Hell was being born before my eyes.

The trouble began when Jerome showed up one morning with the paint. Now I don't profess to know anything about carpentry and even less about paint. But I happened to wander into the cellar as he was preparing his brushes and I glanced at the cans. Two words on the label popped out at me: "oil-based."

I remember having read somewhere that oil-based paints are pretty smelly. And any wine-lover knows that strong scents of any kind are bad for bottles. That's because wine corks are porous, allowing minute quantities of air to penetrate and assist the maturation process. Smelly air can taint the wine – after all, who wants a bottle of Chateau Latour with a background taste of turpentine?

So I said something to Jerome. Wrong paint, I suggested.

Not to worry, Jerome assured me. Because the room was to be refrigerated, an oil-based paint was needed. This type had been especially formulated for these conditions. It would smell for a day or so, that was all.

Still, I worried. So I called Fred.

"Hey, we're experts in this, remember," Fred said reassuringly. "We know what we're doing. Relax."

So I relaxed. What do I know about paint?

Jerome did his work, surveyed it with pride, pronounced the cellar finished, and departed.

The paint stench just about knocked us over when we walked in. But, hey, they said it would be gone in a day or so. In the meantime, my wine bottles remained stored in the spare room.

A week later I called Fred.

"The paint still smells."

"Huh. Must be because it's pretty damp in there. Taking a little longer to dry. Don't worry, it'll soon be gone. Leave the door open to make sure it's well ventilated."

Another week passed. I called Fred.

"It still smells."

"Cedar chips."

"What?"

"Spread some cedar chips in there. Great for absorbing smells. You can get them at any builders' supply."

Our local builders' supply stores don't carry cedar chips. We compromised by buying some cedar eggs, the kind you spread around closets to discourage moths.

Shirley also thought that spreading some dried scented flowers on the floor might help squelch the paint smell.

The result was an aromatic melange which wasn't quite as oppressive as the paint alone. But you sure wouldn't want to put a wine bottle anywhere close to it.

It didn't work. I called Fred.

He sighed. "I said cedar chips. Not cedar eggs. I'll bring them."

He showed up the next day with two giant bags of cedar chips, which he proceeded to dump all over our new wine cellar floor to a depth of about three inches.

"How are we ever going to get rid of them?" my wife whispered.

"We'll worry about that when we get rid of the smell," I whispered back.

Fred finished. "It'll be okay in no time," he said. It was now early June.

You'd think that the smell from a cellar full of cedar chips would overpower any other odour. Not so. Whenever we walked into the wine cellar, all we could smell was the paint. The cedar chips might as well not have been there.

In mid-June I called Fred. It took him a few days to get back to me. I began to suspect I shouldn't have been so prompt with my payment.

"The cedar chips didn't work," I reported when he finally came on the line.

"Well," he said, "Well, well."

At this point I delicately reminded him that I had raised a red flag before the paint ever went on the walls.

"You said it would be okay. Has this ever happened before?"

"Actually, we've never used this paint before."

I stared at the receiver.

"Maybe I'd better talk to the manufacturers," he went on.

"Maybe you'd better," I agreed.

A few days later, Fred arrived with two paint specialists in tow. They entered the cellar.

"It *does* smell," one said. The tone implied he had believed until that moment we were the victims of terminal paint hysteria.

"You've noticed," I said. "How nice. Now do something."

They sniffed. They ran fingers over the walls. They took the temperature of the room. They conferred in whispers. They pronounced.

"Humidity!"

"Humidity," I echoed dumbly.

"The humidity's too high. Paint can't dry properly. Put in a dehumidifier."

We put in our old dehumidifier. It ran day and night. The water basket had to be emptied almost on a hourly basis. They were right on that score. The room was humid.

The overworked dehumidifier broke down. I called Fred.

"We'll send a new one."

He did. It kept pumping moisture out of the air.

The smell remained, strong as ever.

Canada Day had come and gone. The wine bottles were still piled in boxes in the spare room. Every time I wanted a bottle of wine with dinner I had to rummage through several cases to find what I wanted.

I was losing patience.

"Heat," Fred pronounced the next time I reached him.

"Yeah," I agreed. It was over ninety degrees outside. "Does tend to happen in July."

"No, in the cellar," he said. "It'll dry the paint, get rid of the smell. This will work, trust me."

Jerome came with a high-powered electric heater.

"Keep the door closed," he advised. "Let it really bake in there."

It baked. The temperature rose to well over a hundred degrees. For a few days, we were the proud owners of North York's largest oven. The paint loved it. The smell was stronger than ever.

By now I sensed Fred was regarding me as a nuisance. It became increasingly difficult to reach him.

Finally, as July was winding down, I cornered him.

"I've been thinking about your cellar," he began.

So had I – for several months now.

"I think the real problem is ventilation. There are no windows in there, no air movement. So the smell just hangs around."

"So what should I do? Put in a skylight?"

"Have you got a fan?"

"I can get one."

"Set it up in there. Open the door and let it blow. This'll do it. Trust me."

For the first time there was actually some improvement. Not much – certainly not enough to consider moving the wine back in. But a little.

I let the fan keep blowing. But by early August it was clear it wasn't going to be enough.

"You need an industrial strength fan," Fred declared when I reported progress. "Something that will really suck the air out."

"What's that going to cost?"

"Let me talk to the paint people again."

They all came back, went through the same routine, and agreed the smell was still there.

"We want to put a pump in your furnace room and vent it to the outside," the senior specialist said. "That should do it. But we have to knock a few holes in your walls."

Oh. A few holes.

"Don't worry, we won't charge you."

Gee, thanks.

The holes were knocked and the air pump went in. It actually worked – to a degree. But the paint odour lingered on. If the cellar was intended for storing something that didn't care about the stench – such as all the clothes our kids wore once and decided they didn't like – it wouldn't have mattered. But wine? No way.

The paint specialists conferred again and decided there was only one thing left to do.

"Paint it over with urethane. Two coats. It will seal in the smell for good."

"But the urethane will smell worse," I protested.

"That will vanish in no time. Trust us."

What choice did I have? It was now September. The work had started in May, remember?

Jerome came back. He applied the first coat and came staggering out of the cellar, drunk with the fumes.

To his credit, though, he showed up again a few days later and did the second coat.

The stench was awful. But gradually it began to fade. And then one day I walked in and – a miracle! The air was clean!

The refrigeration unit was installed, the racks went up,

the wine came in and by Thanksgiving my new cellar was done. It had only taken five months.

It was wonderful. I was like a kid with a new toy. I spent hours in the fifty-five degree temperature arranging the wines, labelling the bottles, calculating the optimum time for drinking each. Never mind that I was making myself a candidate for pneumonia. For the first time since I'd collected stamps as a kid, I had a real hobby.

Oh, there were a few problems, of course. The refrigeration unit behaved strangely at times, occasionally tripping the circuit breaker. But I didn't pay much attention. Our renovation emphasis had turned elsewhere.

In September, 1991 – about a year after the offending paint smell was finally conquered – I noticed a strange noise from the ventilation fans on the ceiling of the wine cellar. I was about to leave for Lake Louise, Alberta on a speaking engagement, so I mentioned it to Shirley and turned off the system until I could get back and take a look at it.

While I was away, she decided to test it. She flicked on the switch at the master panel in the furnace room. From the adjacent wine cellar, she heard a tremendous crash!

She turned off the refrigeration unit and went in. There, hanging from the ceiling by its electrical cables, was our ventilation fan. One end was balanced precariously on the top of a wine rack holding a six hundred dollar bottle of 1967 Chateau d'Yquem which I'd received as a gift. The other was suspended ominously in mid-air.

She called the refrigeration company. A technician eventually arrived, grumbling about being summoned on a Saturday.

"Couldn't it have waited until Monday?" he complained, as he walked with her down the stairs. "It's probably just a little adjustment and. . .Jesus Christ!"

He had opened the door. He couldn't believe what he saw.

The next few days featured a classic display of finger-pointing.

"Not our fault," the refrigeration people said. "Talk to Fred."

"Not my fault," Fred said. "The refrigeration people installed the unit."

"Not my fault," I told them both. "Just fix it."

Eventually, it was decided that it was indeed *my* fault (well, what else would you expect them to say?). I hadn't put in a properly insulated ceiling. Moisture had gotten in and weakened the old drywall. The bolts holding the fan in place had simply pulled out.

"No one told me we needed a new ceiling," I protested to Fred.

He didn't come out and say I should have known it but there was no mistaking the tone.

"We can do it for you. At cost price. Seven hundred dollars."

"Fine. Just do it."

At this point you may be wondering why I didn't take my business elsewhere. The problem is, wine cellars are a rather specialized field. There aren't many people who build them.

Anyway, Fred assured me they'd never experienced anything like this.

"Ninety-nine point nine per cent of our cellars are perfect, no problems," he said. "It just seems like everything that can possibly go wrong has happened to yours."

He was trying to reassure me. It didn't work. But there was nowhere else to turn.

A new carpenter arrived, Jerome presumably having been sent to whatever purgatory awaits those who use the wrong paint. The new man – we'll call him Ted – turned out to be a great improvement.

He charted all the wines in the cellar – now over four hundred bottles – and carried them back to the spare room. Then he set to work.

The ceiling was in bad shape, no question about it. In

fact, when he probed, it had a consistency similar to oatmeal.

It came down, the new ceiling went up, and that seemed to be it – until his assistant leaned against the wall Jerome had constructed and saw his elbow go through it.

"Oh, Mrs. Pape . . ."

My wife was upstairs in the kitchen when Ted called.

"You'd better come down and take a look at this."

Phone consultations. More finger pointing. Finally, a diagnosis.

The urethane – which by now Ted was peeling off like Saran Wrap – had been a big mistake. Sure, it sealed in the smell. But it also meant the walls couldn't breathe. Moisture from the outside had become trapped in the drywall and couldn't escape. So it accumulated and accumulated some more until, finally, it produced mush.

The new wall was rotten. Actually, I was lucky the racks hadn't pulled away and come crashing down, taking all the bottles with them. I'm not quite sure what I would have done had that happened, besides sitting in the middle of the floor and crying.

Clearly, the wall would have to be rebuilt.

"I'm not paying," I told Fred.

"You won't have to," Fred acknowledged gracefully. "Our fault. But this cellar is costing me a fortune."

Cheap at the price, I thought, as I hung up.

Ted did the job. The wall was rebuilt. Then one morning, he brought in the paint. I looked at the labels. Latex. Fine, I thought.

"There's just one thing," Ted said. "We should try to keep moisture from coming in from outside. I'd like to put a couple of coats of sealant on your front porch."

"Fine," I said, unthinking.

His assistant came the next day and applied the first coat. I went down into the wine cellar.

The stench was overwhelming!

Fortunately, this time it only took a few weeks to get rid

of it. By Christmas the wine cellar was back in full operation.

That was over a year ago. There have been no major problems since.

But sometimes in the night I wake up and think I hear something down there, working away, preparing the next disaster.

Don't be so foolish, I tell myself, and roll over.

I'm sure that's not a sadistic chuckle I hear from the bowels of the house just before I drift off.

Buy a Dog, Fix It Up

I sometimes think Shirley has a masochistic streak. How else can you explain her involvement with The Dog?

Having gone through the trauma of renovating our own house, I'd have thought she'd be content to sit back, relax, and rest on her laurels. I should have known better. Like Alexan-

der the Great, she's always looking for new worlds to con-
quer.

Kim presented her with the opportunity. She and her
husband, Tim, were living in a one-bedroom apartment
which was all right for them but totally inadequate for the
baby that was on the way.

After thinking it over for about thirty seconds, Kim came
up with the solution – they'd buy a house.

There was just one small problem. They didn't have any
money.

Well, very little anyway. They had a few thousand
dollars in RRSPs, which they could tap into through the federal
government's temporary Home Buyers' Plan. They'd also put
a bit into the Ontario Home Ownership Plan and had a small
savings account. Still, added all together, it wasn't nearly
enough for a down payment.

So they came to see me. After all, what are fathers for?
I crunched their numbers in the computer, worked out how
much Shirley and I could throw in, figured out their maximum
monthly payment and came up with a price target. If they
could find a place for under a hundred and sixty thousand,
they could just swing it.

Even in the midst of Toronto's housing slump, there
wasn't much available at that price – certainly not in desirable
locations.

About all our real estate agent could find were condo-
minium town houses – and even they tended to be priced at
one seventy-five and up.

The kids looked at a few they liked but they were too
expensive. The ones that were cheap enough were either
falling down or too far from public transportation (they didn't
own a car). They were starting to get discouraged; then they
saw The Dog.

They gave it that name from the first viewing. It was a
well-located house about a mile from our place with lots of
green space, three bedrooms, two bathrooms, two fireplaces,
a rec room, and a fine view over the city. The asking price was
well below anything else they'd looked at. That's because it

had one serious flaw. It was an interior designer's worst nightmare come true.

Normally, a renovated home should command a higher price. This place was a classic example of how a bad renovation can end up costing its owners thousands of dollars.

I don't know who the culprits were. It may have been the people who were offering the house for sale or it may have been some previous occupant. But somewhere along the way, someone had decided to impose his own peculiar tastes on the house, with disastrous results. I suspect it was a retiree with time on his hands and delusions of carpentry competence.

Mere words can't do justice to the scale of tastelessness we found but take a walk with me through the house and I'll do my best.

Let's go in the front door. Notice the red padded vinyl that's been applied to the inside as it closes behind us. If you look closely, you'll see it's been affixed with brass-headed tacks.

We're now in the main hall. Take a look at the floor; you'll see that four different types of peel and stick tiles have been used, none of them complementary.

Here's the small downstairs bathroom. Interesting idea, carpeting it in gold shag. There must have been some left over because they continued it up one wall. How do you like the cherry-red plastic stick-on tiles? Oh, and you see that piece of dark wood panelling? There's actually a window behind that. Apparently, they didn't like light.

Yes, we wondered about that bucket under the drain pipe too.

This is the kitchen. Dark wooden cupboards accented by artificial red brick facing on the walls with some fake oak panelling tossed in for effect. Note the recently-added drop ceiling that cuts about two feet from the height of the room. There's a mass of purposeless wiring above it, along with some red flock wallpaper.

It's a short stroll from here to the dining and living rooms with their relatively new cherry-red wall-to-wall carpeting.

Someone *really* liked red; it shows up all through the house. Yes, there's hardwood floor underneath the carpet. No, you don't want to look at it. It's been stained so badly with dog urine that not even a professional floor restorer can do anything with it.

Notice that all the walls have been finished in deeply stained plywood panelling. Keeps the rooms nice and dark. To heighten the effect, someone has glued brown foam beams to the ceilings and to the fireplace. The only decorating reference point we can think of is Olde English pub.

You'll also notice the many jerry-built cupboards that have been added, plus that strange-looking home-made entertainment unit partially blocking off the living room entrance. No, I'm not sure what all those hanging wires are for.

Let's go downstairs. The house is built on a slope so the rec room looks out over a garden. At least, it would if it had any windows. There was a window over there once. It's now been filled in with a room air conditioner. Rather odd, because this should be the coolest room in the house, yet it's the only one with an air conditioner. There's a door to the patio over there. It's solid; no glass. Looks like a dungeon, you say? Funny, we thought the same thing.

You'll notice there are three different colours of dark stained panels on the walls. I'd rather you didn't open any of those home-made cabinets. They're filled with scrap wood.

I hope you like shag carpeting because the floor has a combination of two different colours – lime green and orange.

Those bullfight and matador pictures on all the walls? The owners will include them in the price. You're welcome.

Let's go up to the bedroom level. Here's some more gold shag carpeting on the stairs. Yes, the hardwood underneath is actually in decent shape.

This is the master bedroom. I agree, it does seem rather bright when compared to the downstairs. Orange-red walls, wood panelling and red and gold velour wallpaper on the cupboard doors will do it every time. Nice view. I'm a bit surprised they didn't block in the window.

Here's the second bedroom. Note the giant floor-to-ceiling cabinet built of plywood. Great for storage. Well, yes, it does reduce the size of the room by about a quarter, but hey – you have to give up something to get something.

Now this third bedroom will be great for the baby. Let's just hope he or she likes turquoise velour wallpaper.

Finally, the main bathroom. I hope you don't mind gold shag carpeting where a medicine cabinet mirror would normally be. The use of artificial red brick as a backsplash to the basin? Well, it's. . . interesting. And here are some more of those wonderful cherry-red plastic tiles lining the bath and shower area.

What did you say? Someone certainly has unusual taste? Well, yes, we thought so too.

The house was empty when Kim and Tim looked at it – perhaps the owners couldn't take it any more; in any event they had long gone. It had been on the market for several months with no takers. As a result, the price had been knocked down at least twice.

"It sounds like a great fixer-upper," I said. It was fine for me to talk. I hadn't seen the place and if anybody was going to get involved in fixing-upping, it sure wasn't going to be me.

"I'll have a look," Shirley said.

She returned somewhat glassy-eyed.

"Well, it *is* a challenge," she acknowledged. "But I think it's manageable."

On that basis, the rebuilding of ancient Troy is probably also "manageable". It's all a matter of time, energy and money.

I went to see for myself. Yes, the place had potential. Certainly, if it had been in decent shape it would have been well out of the kids' price range. But the renovations would cost a small fortune.

"No, they won't," Shirley said. "I know ways to do it."

Sure, by knocking it down and starting over, I thought. But I kept silent. This was her area of expertise, not mine.

So the kids talked to their agent and put in an offer. It was well below the already reduced asking price.

The selling agent haggled. The owners can't accept such

a low bid, we were told.

"They'd rather keep paying upkeep on an empty house nobody but a fool would touch with a barge pole?" I said.

We offered one thousand more. Our agent in effect told them to take it or leave it.

They took it. I was pleased because the kids got a good price. I was unhappy because they were now stuck with someone else's mess.

A few weeks later, Kim and Tim took possession of The Dog. I lost my wife.

At least, I lost her for two months. Every waking hour she spent at The Dog. Because the kids were on a tight budget, they didn't have the luxury of turning the whole project over to a contractor. This was do-it-yourself time.

Everyone was pressed into service. Shirley acted as general contractor and decorating adviser, with assistance from Beth. Tim took on the role of The Wrecker, tearing down panelling, pulling off the fake beams, stripping wallpaper, ripping out the rickety built-ins. Kim, almost eight months pregnant at this point, looked after light cleaning and sweeping up. Deborah and some of Kim's friends were pressed into painting service on their days off. Me? I visited occasionally and made helpful comments. At least, *I* thought they were helpful.

The Dog did its best to defeat them. Tim discovered that the handyman who had put up the panelling had been careful never to use one nail where ten would do. He'd also purchased what appeared to be the world's longest nails; we were amazed to find they hadn't penetrated through the outside walls.

Every layer that was removed revealed another problem beneath. The living room panelling covered a dark, imitation wood wallpaper, which in turn covered a wall with so many holes it looked as if it had been riddled by machine gun fire. We wondered exactly what had gone on in the house before we took it over.

The foam beams appeared to have been attached to the ceiling with black rubber cement, which left behind a dark, sticky residue that had to be scraped away.

The same material also seemed to have been used as the adhesive to attach the shag carpeting to the walls. Tim got the shag off but the downstairs bathroom was left in such a mess that new drywall was the only alternative.

By the time the wrecking phase was finished, there were three thousand pounds worth of someone's idea of home beautification piled in the living room (we know because we had to pay by weight to have it hauled to the dump).

Someone with execrable taste had spent a small fortune to decorate the place – and then lost thousands more on the sale price of the house as a result. There's a lesson there somewhere.

Grudgingly, reluctantly, The Dog succumbed. It was something like an archaeological project. Hours of work finally unearthed the original walls. More hours, and the holes were filled in and smoothed off. The drywall absorbed paint as if it had never been touched by it before. First a base, then a coat, then another coat, then, in some cases, yet another coat.

The rooms became bright again.

Shirley hired a carpenter to install a sliding glass patio door in the rec room. Suddenly, the whole garden opened up.

Soft pastels replaced the reds and turquoises in the bedrooms. At Beth's suggestion, the red brick and tile in the main bathroom was painted white. It took five coats, but it worked.

The shag on the stairs disappeared and some intensive scrubbing brought out the natural colour of the wood.

The bullfighters went into the trashcan. So did the maze of unexplained overhead wires, which even an electrician was unable to sort out.

A new hall closet was built to fill in the scar left by the demolished entertainment unit. The fireplace was cleaned, the covered windows thrown open, the hall tiles re-covered in a black and white checkerboard pattern, the red vinyl padding on the doors discarded.

It took about twice as long as Shirley had expected. But

every finished room brought a new sense of accomplishment. They pushed ahead.

Ten days after the new baby was born, the kids were able to move in. The house sparkled.

If I hadn't witnessed the transformation myself, I wouldn't have believed it.

The neighbours who visited marvelled at the change. So did the real estate agent, who suggested they put it back on the market and make a big profit.

The kids didn't even think twice before saying no.

The Dog was gone. They had a home.

How We'll Do It Next Time

This chapter is probably misnamed. I don't expect there will ever be a next time. Having lived through a complete home renovation once, I hope I won't ever have to again.

But if we *should* ever renovate another home, there's a lot I think we'd do differently – and a few things we'd do in exactly the same way.

Shirley doesn't like making lists so I've made one for her, just in case. If I ever come in for breakfast some morning and see it attached to the refrigerator door, I know I'm in trouble.

Here it is:

1) Plan, plan, plan. I know it's dull. Working out detailed schedules, poring over diagrams, setting and sticking to budgets, spending hours shopping for mundane items like sinks and toilets. All I can tell you is that the alternative is worse, unless you happen to enjoy chaos.

2) Rely on the inevitability of Murphy's Law. After all that time spent planning, it's natural to assume all the pieces will fall into place. Materials will be available when required, tradespeople will show up on time, bad weather will never intervene. Your tile man won't be called for jury duty, unexpected visitors won't arrive and the paint won't smell. Maybe you'll be lucky. Maybe nothing at all will go wrong. Just don't count on it.

3) Keep a sense of humour. Okay, so I wasn't amused when Misha ran through the paint tray. At least, not at that moment. But now when I go out on the deck and see those fading white paw prints, I can chuckle. And we've dined out many times on the wine cellar and groundhog stories. Life's too short to be up-tight. So when something goes awry – as it will – look on the funny side and think how many free meals it will be worth.

4) Don't try to do everything at once. When I told Shirley I expected the renovations would take three years, she looked at me in disbelief. Actually, they took more than four and it's a good thing. Can you imagine all those disasters happening in the space of six months? At least by spreading them out we were able to retain a measure of perspective. Some people have told me they'd prefer to have the whole job over and done with in a couple of months. Usually, they're people who've never actually tried doing it that way. Those who have almost invariably say: "Never again." For your own sanity, and the sake of your budget, do it in stages – with some long pauses in between.

5) Use an interior designer. If the job's a big one, get some professional help. It will probably save you time and money in the long run. Personal references are the best way to find a designer. Before you make a choice, interview two or three. Ask about their qualifications, whether they are members of professional associations that have codes of ethics, and how they charge for their services. If you can figure that one out, you're one up on me.

6) Get several quotes. Never contract a job without getting a number of quotes first. Go over them carefully to see exactly what's included and what's not; make sure you're comparing apples and apples. If possible, try to get a firm price, not just an estimate. Estimates have a way of escalating rapidly, especially in the construction trades. Your quote should also include a time frame for starting and completing the job; if it doesn't, ask for one. If you use an interior designer, he or she should be able to suggest tradespeople you may want to consult but you're also free to select your own.

7) Get it in writing. When you've made a choice, get all the terms of the deal in writing. That way, if the shower keeps leaking, you can be reasonably sure someone will do something about it.

8) Withhold ten per cent of the final payment until a month after completion. This is an even more effective way of ensuring any problems will be promptly attended to. The tradespeople won't like it but it's your house and your money.

9) Budget for more. Whatever the quote, add more to it for your personal budgeting – twenty-five per cent is a good rule of thumb. You'll almost certainly end up spending it, and if you don't, it's money in the bank. That way, when the floor man comes to you and says the wood that was included in the estimate is too thin and likely to warp (as happened to us), you'll have some money in reserve to ensure the work is done right.

10) Use local people. Wherever possible, try to use tradespeople from your immediate area. If they feel there's a possibility for repeat business later, they may make a special effort to please you.

11) When you find a good tradesperson, hang on. Good carpenters, electricians, plumbers and painters are hard to come by. If you encounter one or more during your renovations, get a name and phone number before they leave. In most cases, they're independents, working on a sub-contract basis, so they'll be available for future business. Even if they are employed full time by a contractor, you may find they're willing to moonlight on small jobs.

12) Triple-check delivery dates. Promises are fine but there's a direct relationship between the length of time from the commitment date to the delivery date. The longer the gap, the greater the likelihood of a foul-up. Call a week before to make sure everything's still on track; then call again the day before. Don't worry about being branded a pest. Better that than paying tradespeople to sit on their hands because materials didn't arrive when promised.

13) Don't make over the kitchen in the winter. Next to a bathroom, the kitchen is the most indispensable room in your home. If you have do be without it for any length of time, make sure it's in the summer when your barbecue and salads can take up the slack.

14) Be persistent. Most of us don't know a lot about construction techniques or materials. That's what we hire professionals for. But occasionally, common sense warns us that something isn't quite as it should be. When that happens, get pushy. Insist on proper explanations before things go any farther. Think what would have happened if I'd laid down the law and said there would be no oil-based paint in my wine cellar. No disaster. No book chapter.

15) Don't do it yourself unless you're good. A good home renovation can add tens of thousands of dollars to the value of your home. A bad one can subtract just as much. If you're skilled at the work and have good taste, go to it. Otherwise, hire professionals or forget the whole thing. If you're bored, play bridge.

16) Buy quality. Yes, it costs more, whether it's cabinets, appliances or faucets. But, in the long term, it costs less. Take furniture. There's a lot of cheap stuff on the market. Tim and Kim bought some shortly after they were married because it was all they thought they could afford. Within three years, the chair was broken and the sofa had become so soft it was like sitting on a mound of feathers. Shirley's thirty-year-old Krohler chesterfield was in better shape, and we disposed of it. If you can't afford to buy quality new, then buy it second-hand. You'll come out better in the long run.

One final thought. You've undoubtedly read articles about which home renovations have the biggest payoff in terms of adding to the re-sale value of your property. I've even written a few myself.

But this is *your* home we're talking about. What really matters is how comfortable *you* are with the end result. What's the point of having a house that's worth more money if you're not happier with it than you were before?

Many of us define our happiness by our families and our homes. They are a true reflection of our personal values and our perceptions of the world.

If you decide that you want to make over your home some day, do it with that thought in mind. Make sure the final result reflects you and your desires. Don't spend a lot of money creating someone else's dream.